After the Cheering Stops

A Retirement Game Plan
for Elite Athletes
and Baby Boomer Career Professionals
Seeking a New Future

by Alan Spector

Also by Alan Spector

Baseball: Never Too Old to Play "The" Game

Hail Hail to U City High

Your Retirement Quest
(with coauthor Keith Lawrence)

University City Schools: Our First 100 Years

Body Not Recovered

www.aaspector.com

ISBN-13: 978-1984036957
ISBN-10: 1984036955

Cover Photo: "The Allure of an Empty Ballpark" by Susan Petrone

Dedication

To Keith Lawrence, friend and business partner—without your inspiration to understand retirement and share out learning, neither *Your Retirement Quest* nor *After the Cheering Stops* would have happened.

Acknowledgments

As always, thanks to my wife, Ann, my first beta reader and my forever cheerleader.

Speaking of beta readers, you are the best—thank you to Jill Chapin, friend and classmate; to Julie Isphording, who challenged me to lean into the future; to Don Davey, who leant both his athletic and financial experience to the project; to Pete Woods, who dedicated his precious time to dig into the details; and to Jerry Reuss, Ken Holtzman, Kim Ensing, Jonathan Miller, Dan Batsch, and Garrett Broshuis, all who care deeply about helping athletes transition into retirement.

Thank you also to the other athlete and sports-related interviewees, Cindy Rarick, Dan Cross, Janna LaCock, and Leigh Steinberg.

So many others contributed—thank you to all of you: Larry Murphy for your efforts to connect me with Jimmy Connors; Mike Ferrari for connecting me with Dan Cross, Mary Carlson for connecting me with Cindy Rarick; Alice Faintich, Marshall Faintich, and Arleen Bly for helping build the book's concept; Jack Powell for guidance on the book's title; Jim Hopkins for his wisdom and insight about the unifying principle of the book and for the cover design; Ken Ruettgers for providing me with his dissertation, *Barriers to NFL Career Transition*; Tom Ackerman for his continuing counsel and encouragement; Vince Gennaro and Jacob Pomrenke, the SABR folks who do what SABR folks do—providing data and insight; and Carol Strelic and Betsy Clark for helping me think about grief management.

Thank you to Mike Souders and Michael Barnes for believing in the project and sharing it with others and to Michele McManamon, Howard Richards, Andy Limbaugh, and Ken Mares for recognizing the import of the book's content and considering it as integrative to their great work.

Table of Contents

Introduction

Introduction

---

*"They teach you how to play the game,
but they don't teach you how to leave it."*
Gordie Howe

---

*"(Jackie Robinson) said that athletes die twice.
You know, when the first career is gone, that's a death."*
Kareem Abdul-Jabbar

The transition into and through retirement is fraught with risk. You have passionately dedicated your life to the pursuit of a single dream, achieving at the highest level. In many ways, your career has been all-consuming.

Your identity, self-esteem, and perhaps even life purpose have been defined by your career and your achievements. As an elite athlete, relationships have revolved around teammates, coaches, reporters, fans, and the entourage, and life has been structured by workout and practice regimens, by travel schedules, and by games, meets, matches, and tournaments.

As a non-athlete, relationships have revolved around colleagues, students, patients, and clients, and life has been structured by work and travel schedules, by requests from the boss, and by deadlines, reports, meetings, and business cycles.

Then one day, as an athlete, whether by your choice, by a coach's or general manager's decision, or because of injury, your typically short college, professional, or Olympic career is over. Or as a non-athlete, whether by choice, by a boss's or company's decision, or because of health issues, your long career is over.

What's next? What happens *After the Cheering Stops*?

Marilyn Monroe, who while she was married to New York Yankee legend, Joe DiMaggio, returned from a tour of Korea during which she was greeted enthusiastically, as you might imagine, by the troops for whom she was performing. Upon returning home, she reported to DiMaggio, "Oh Joe, you never heard such cheering."

Joe coldly responded, "Oh, yes I have."

New York Jets quarterback, Joe Namath, made a similar point in his own way, "Ever been cheered? Ever heard 60,000 people chanting your name? It's indescribable, man. Heck, even the booing doesn't sound bad...I understand why actors like to work in front of a live audience. The applause...applause...applause."

In his autobiography, *Racing the Sunset*, retired professional triathlete, Scott Tinley wrote, "...other ventures in life...cannot replace the immediate closeness and gratification of applause, and once this is gone, an athlete enters the netherworld of being forgotten."

Tinley won the Ironman, the world's premier triathlon, in 1982 and again in 1985, the first year prize money, albeit inconsequential, was awarded. Although he had sponsorships that enabled him to focus on his sport full time, Tinley was far from what we think of today as a highly paid professional athlete.

By contrast, former three-time NFL Pro-Bowl player, Tiki Barber, had an estimated $35,000,000 in career earnings. Yet Barber's statement about his retirement transition sounds eerily similar to Tinley's, "I realized how fast the opportunities disappear. You've been replaced on the field and you've been replaced in people's minds. That's when you start getting depressed."

Although these are examples from the sports world, elite athletes and their non-athlete counterparts share the challenges of the major and inevitable transition into and through retirement. There are some who adjust gracefully and discover their new life path. Many others struggle to find their way. Some never do.

It doesn't take much searching to find studies and a multitude of media reports that use words like "depression," "divorce," "bankruptcy," "disability," and even "suicide" with regard to retired elite athletes, Baby Boomers, and others.

These are frightening issues, but even for those who are fortunate enough not to have to deal with concerns as drastic, the transition from career to retirement can be difficult. For the elite athlete, that retirement timeframe might begin in your 20s or 30s. For the non-athlete, it might begin in your 50s, 60s, or 70s. Regardless, the question you should and could be asking now is, "What is my game plan to increase the odds of winning in retirement; being happy and fulfilled for my remaining years?"

Or we can return to the original questions, "What's next? What happens *After the Cheering Stops*?"

Because the key to answering these questions, similar to the key to winning a game or closing a business deal, is having a strong game plan, you'll find the book's structure to follow this familiar athletic construct:

➢ The Playing Field: understanding what retirement is and what it isn't and discovering what are its challenges and opportunities

➢ The Game Plan: enhancing retirement by understanding and leveraging personal strengths, by identifying and acting on personal improvement opportunities, by creating a customized retirement game plan, and by building a retirement team

➢ Practicing: learning when, how, and why to practice the retirement game plan while still playing or working and deciding when to retire on one's own terms

➢ Playing the Game: understanding how to recognize changing life circumstances and make game plan adjustments, and knowing how to play to win

The concepts, tools, and techniques in *After the Cheering Stops* derive from two primary sources. First, over the past decade, my friend, business partner, and coauthor, Keith Lawrence, and I have been studying and sharing, primarily with Baby Boomers, how to increase the odds of living a fulfilling retirement. Many thousands have read our book, *Your Retirement Quest,* and attended our workshops. The vast majority of what we have learned and shared applies to elite athletes as well.

Second, I've had the opportunity to review relevant research and media reports regarding the risks elite athletes face in retirement and to gain insights from interviews with many retired elite athletes and others in the sports world. You'll find their perspectives and profiles throughout the book.

In general, here's what those who are retiring from all-consuming careers tend to face. Both elite athletes and their non-athlete counterparts are largely unaware of the challenges and opportunities that lie ahead. Individuals in both groups are largely unprepared for what may be the most significant transition of their lives. Those that have done any planning have focused almost exclusively on their finances. Yet, winning in retirement derives from a game plan that includes an integrated approach to financial security and a rich and diverse portfolio of meaningful activities.

With that in mind, put yourself in a locker room where you are about to get a pre-game message from your coach—in this case, your retirement coach. You may be an elite athlete, an executive, a professional dancer, an attorney, a teacher, a military officer, or anyone else who has been fully dedicated to a career. You may be a 24-year old Olympian or the 55-year old engineer or the 40-year old major league pitcher or the 58-year old high school principal or the 21-year old collegiate linebacker or the 65-year old medical professional. Regardless, this is what you might, and perhaps should, hear.

"You're having a successful career and have built the skills to become the winner you are. People recognize what you've accomplished. You know, however, that there will come a time when your career will end. You may choose that time; it may be chosen by others; or circumstances may dictate it. What are you doing now to get ready?

"You can prepare for that inevitable and significant life transition by thinking about how you have achieved success in your current career. You learned from coaches, mentors, and the veterans, those who had gone before you, about the challenges you'd need to deal with and the opportunities you could pursue. You envisioned the future you wanted to create, set goals along the way, and established plans to best attain what you wanted to accomplish. You looked within yourself to know your own strengths and weaknesses—you built on those strengths, addressed your weak spots, honed your skills through learning and practice, and made sure you had a good team to support you. And you recognized and adjusted to changing circumstances.

"The good news is that those are exactly the steps we're going to take together to help you prepare for retirement. You've worked hard to get where you are, and, similarly, you will benefit from an investment of time and effort to create the future you deserve.

"Winning in retirement comes from preparing, planning, practicing, partnering and then playing, just as it has in your career. So, let's start now to make sure you win, even *After the Cheering Stops*."

Alan Spector

The Playing Field

When athletes prepare for competition, they make sure to know everything they can about the conditions in which they will be playing. Which way is the wind blowing? How strong is it? Is the field, course, track, ice, or pitch soft or hard, and how does that play to their strengths and weaknesses? What is the temperature? Will there be shadows and, if so, where? How much of the course will be uphill and at which mile-markers will the tough hills be? Answers to these questions and others help determine, "What's my game plan to take all of this into account and increase the odds that I'll win?"

When athletes prepare for retirement, they should also know about the conditions in which they will be living. What are the challenges they may face? Where are the tough hills? Which way is the wind blowing and how strong? Are there aspects that play to their strengths? Answers to these questions and others help determine, "What's my game plan to take all of this into account and increase the odds that I'll win in retirement?"

You guessed it—the same thought process applies as well to retiring non-athletes who have been passionate about and fully-committed to their careers.

These first three chapters of the book are intended to describe the retirement playing field, focusing on understanding its challenges and the phases you will go through as you transition beyond your career. Full awareness of retirement's "playing field" will go a long way toward helping you create a better game plan for your future.

Chapter 1

Retirement is the Wrong Word

---

*"I've got a lot of years to live after baseball,
and I would like to live them with complete use of my body."*
Sandy Koufax

"Life doesn't stop with football."
Barry Sanders

What do these people have in common with each other and with you?

➢ Sandy Koufax retired at age 30 after a Hall-of-Fame career, during which he earned four World Series rings and three Cy Young awards and threw four no-hitters and a perfect game.

➢ Risa Sreden Prince retired at age 55 after closing her horse and cargo trailer business. Risa built the business to a point where she could say, "It took me many years to become an overnight success." But a success she did become...both in making the business profitable and in knowing when to walk away.

➢ Annika Sorenstam retired at age 39 after winning 72 LPGA tournaments, including ten majors, and being named player of the year eight times in her 16-year career.

➢ Keith Lawrence retired at age 53 from a 32-year career as Human Resources executive and was considered a worldwide organization development thought leader, both inside and outside his company.

➢ Jim Brown retired at age 29 after an eight-year NFL career, during which he was a three-time MVP and for which in 2002, *Sporting News* named him the greatest football player of all time.

➢ Arleen White Bly retired at age 64 from a 24-year career as an educator, having gained the respect of other faculty, staff, parents, and most importantly, her students. When she retired, she was a staff developer, helping bring leading-edge educational ideas to her colleagues.

➢ Mark Spitz retired at age 22 having earned nine swimming gold medals, seven of them in one Olympics, one silver, and one bronze.

➢ Tim Arnold retired at age 66 from a colorful 40-year career in the advertising business that included launching the history-making campaign "This Bud's for You," producing the notorious first GoDaddy Super Bowl commercial, and writing extensively for *Adweek* magazine.

It may appear that there are relatively few similarities among this group of people other than they all had successful and all-consuming careers about which they were passionate, and from which they are now retired. Yet they have more in common than may be obvious. We'll talk about the similarities and differences between and among the retirement of elite athletes and their older non-athlete counterparts. For now, consider that each retiring athlete, whether ending a college, professional, or Olympic career, and each of the nearly 10,000 others who retire every day makes perhaps the biggest transition they will ever face in their lives and then decide how to meaningfully spend their retirement years, regardless of how long that might be.

Since you are reading this book, you may have already retired, are seriously considering it in your near future, or are one of the fortunate ones who knows the time is right to start preparing for retirement, regardless of where you are in your career journey. Making the right decision if and when to retire, how to best manage the transition, and how to plan to live the full and fulfilling retirement you deserve starts with understanding more about what retirement is and what it is not.

"Retirement" is the Wrong Word

When you search the dictionary and thesaurus for the word "retirement," you'll find negative connotations. Synonyms are "withdrawal," "departure," "leaving," and "retreat." One definition reads, "...a state of being withdrawn from the rest of the world or from a former busy life." These give retirement a sense of ending rather than beginning.

Yet, retiring from your primary career is not merely an act of ending, but, more opportunistically and relevant, an act of commencement and of the promise of a meaningful future. I sought to find a word to better reflect the optimism of this next phase of life. There were many words and phrases that have been conjured up, but in the end, I decided to use "retirement" anyway. Why? The word is well established in the lexicon, and it serves well to describe a "time" in our lives, albeit not the "condition" of our lives.

With that in mind, throughout this book, let's keep in mind the word's limitations. Our mutual intent is to envision the future such that when we read, hear, or use the word "retirement," we think not of "withdrawal," but of "opportunity;" not of "departure," but of "fulfillment;" not of "retreat," but of "engagement."

Consider Peyton Manning's words from his March 2016 retirement speech, during which, at age 38, he announced the end of his 18-year Hall-of-Fame NFL career. We hope that his sentiments play out for him, and we should all strive for them to be meaningful in our lives as well. He said, "I'm totally convinced that the end of my football career is just the beginning of something I haven't even discovered yet. Life is not shrinking for me, it's morphing into a whole new world of possibilities."

The Longevity Opportunity (and Challenge)

The history of retirement is relevant for both Baby Boomers and elite athletes. Much of how we, as a society, think about retirement today was established by the Prussian/German statesman Chancellor Otto Von Bismarck in the latter half of the 19th century. Being besieged politically, Bismarck sought to regain popular support by declaring that his government would pay a pension to any non-working German over the age of 65. His policy did two things. First, it set the arbitrary world standard for retirement age that has generally stood the test of time. Secondly, it assured the German government would pay few pensions—less than one percent of Germans lived to be 65 at the time.

Longevity has been growing ever since. The average life expectancy in the United States at the time of Bismarck's social program was about 45 years. By 1935, when Social Security was enacted, the average had risen to 60. When AARP was founded in 1958, average life expectancy was approaching 68 and today has grown to approximately 80. And someone living to 62, the approximate average retirement age in the U. S. as of this writing, can now expect to live into their mid-80s.

The steep rise in life expectancy in only the last 50 years has changed the nature of retirement for older retirees, Baby Boomers for example. In the Bismarck era, one could not expect to retire. Boomers can now expect to live 20 to 30 years or more in retirement. One way to think about this is that they may have 7,500 to 11,000 or more days to make the most of this next life phase—the new demographics are an opportunity for a new perspective on what retirement life should and could be.

The situation for athletes is much different statistically but the same conceptually. One source indicates that average Major League Baseball, National Hockey League, National Basketball Association, and National Football League careers are 5.6, 5.5, 4.8, and 3.5 years, respectively. Some argue they are higher than that—so for the sake of this discussion, let's say the average length of career for all is 6.0 years. The average age when players begin their MLB, NHL, NBA, and NFL careers is the low 20s. Again, for the sake of our calculation, let's say the average age of a rookie across all the sports is 22.

Conservatively, therefore, the average retirement age for a professional athlete in the four primary North American team sports is 28. Athletes in the major individual sports (i.e. tennis and golf) tend to retire later as do many Olympic athletes, although in some Olympic sports, retirement can often occur in the early 20s or even younger.

Also consider that the vast majority of athletes who have passionately dedicated their youth to their sport will never play at the professional or Olympic level. In essence, these elite athletes, for indeed that's what they are, retire from their sports careers after college, at age 21 or 22.

If we extrapolate across all of this, it would be fair to say that the average elite athlete retires in his or her early 20s. Those who go on to professional or Olympic careers, retire, on average, by age 30. Athletes, therefore, could have 50 or 60 or more years post-retirement.

Let's use the St. Louis Cardinals Cy Young Award-winning pitcher, Chris Carpenter, as an example. Carpenter retired at the ripe-old athletic age of 38. If we assume that the longevity curve continues to go up, let's say that the average will be 85 by the time he reaches that age. Carpenter's retirement could be 47 years or more—more than 17,000 days.

Think of the possibilities of having 20,000-ish or more days to make the rest of your life the best of your life. Yes, there will also be challenges, and we'll describe them in this section of the book, but not with the intent of making retirement seem unattractive. Rather, we'll address the retirement transition risks to ensure acknowledge and address the realities that we may face and that we need to consider while developing our retirement game plan.

Retiring to Something

How can we think about retirement in this new way—not merely an act of ending but more opportunistically and relevant, an act of commencement and of the promise of a long and meaningful future? Said another way, "How can we think not about retiring from something but retiring to something?"

Let's return to our original list of retirees.

➤ Sandy Koufax retired from his major league career to stay close to the game as a broadcaster, minor league pitching coach, and a member of the advisory board for the Baseball Assistance Team, helping former players through financial and medical difficulties.

➤ Risa Sreden Prince retired from her trailer business to pursue her passion of creating fused glass art.

➤ Annika Sorenstam retired from the LPGA tour to create her foundation to teach children the importance of living a healthy, active lifestyle through fitness and nutrition and to establish the Annika Academy, teaching golf around the world.

➤ Keith Lawrence retired from his Human Resources career to follow his life purpose of "enabling dreams," by coaching individuals, consulting for companies, and by helping friends and family to fulfill their aspirations.

➤ Jim Brown retired from the NFL to act in 44 films and to found the Amer-I-Can Program to help kids caught up in the gang scene in Los Angeles and Cleveland learn life-management skills.

➤ Arleen White Bly retired from teaching to dedicate her time to her friends and family, especially her grandchildren.

➤ Mark Spitz retired from competitive swimming to found a successful real estate company and to enjoy sailing, skiing, and collecting art.

➤ Tim Arnold retired as an advertising executive to become a marketing consultant, write the Foreword for my book, *Hail Hail to U City High* (thanks again, Tim), blog for *The Huffington Post*, cofound The Barn at Sundial Farm, an eclectic home furnishing store, and co-write two novels with best-selling author James Patterson.

Was the transition always smooth? Was the path always direct? No. But the importance of finding new directions in their lives helped each stay the course of retiring not just from something but to something.

Julie Isphording
Olympic Marathoner
"It's hell in the hallway"

Julie Isphording is one of the many retired elite athletes who were kind enough to lend their time, energy, and insights to help me develop the key concepts for this book. You'll find their personal profiles throughout the book in sections where their experiences are most instructive.

Julie is perhaps a poster child for an athlete's successful post-career transition. She struggled with the loss of her sport and all that it afforded her, but she applied what she had learned during her career to create an even more fulfilling life thereafter.

The marathon was born in 490 BC, when the messenger, Pheidippides, ran to Athens to announce victory over Persia in the Battle of Marathon.

Pheidippides is said to have given word of the Athenian victory with his last vestige of energy before falling dead after his 26.2-plus mile run.

The modern Olympic marathon began in 1896 as a male-only event and stayed that way until 1984, by which time the international running community had become more accepting of the very idea of a women's marathon. An Australian, Adrienne Beames, broke the three-hour barrier in 1971, and a year later, the Boston Marathon officially opened to women. In 1979, Norwegian Grete Waitz beat 2:30 in the New York City Marathon. Women marathoners gained even more credibility when Nike supported them in full-page ads in running magazines.

The tide had turned, and the Women's Olympic marathon was approved for the 1984 games in Los Angeles. The United States team was comprised of Joan Benoit, who would win the race at 2:24:52, finishing more than a minute ahead of Waitz, who had never before lost a marathon she had completed, Julie Brown, and a little-known and unexpected team qualifier, Julie Isphording.

Not surprisingly, Isphording was thrilled to be on the team and to be rooming with Mary Lou Retton, surrounded by the best of the best. But the Olympic marathon did not end well for Julie. Running with the lead pack just before the 11-mile mark, her foot collapsed and down she went. The ambulance ride was only the beginning of a valiant comeback that included a diagnosis of a disc problem, back surgery, doctors telling her she would never run again, rigorous rehab, and a return to extensive training. Six years later, on the same course on which her Olympic dreams were dashed, Julie won the Los Angeles marathon in 2:32.

Injuries eventually caught up with her again. In 1999, at the age of 37, Julie was interviewed by the *Cincinnati Enquirer* and said, "I'd love to be able to compete again, but competition is kind of retired to me, and I use the word 'kind of' because the idea of not competing is hard to accept."

Although she is a believer that when one door closes, another opens. Julie quickly points out that sometimes while searching for the right open door, "It's hell in the hallway."

She describes her transition as a time that took her from a life of balance to one of being out of balance. While competing, she was bolstered by the rigor and structure of her sport, by the adulation of her Olympian status, and by the clarity that came from knowing who she was and what her role was in life. When the competitive career ended, Julie, like so many elite athletes, struggled to redefine herself and figure out how to live her new life.

This is where Julie's story becomes so instructive and in essence, establishes the foundation for the remainder of the book. To her credit, Julie chose to reapply the characteristics that enabled her to achieve and regain elite athlete performance. She attributes her successful second life to valuing practice and trusting the process to deliver results; to maintaining optimism, a positive attitude, and the ability to continue in the face of adversity; to accepting failure, knowing we live in a world of second and third chances, and demonstrating resiliency; to seeking out and valuing good coaching, surrounding yourself with the best people, and trusting yourself and others to be good teammates; and to being willing to stretch yourself to the point of vulnerability and humbleness, knowing that is the foundation of improvement.

In retirement, she has been a marketing manager, award-winning syndicated radio host, national keynote speaker, magazine columnist, author of three books, a leadership and training consultant for Fortune 500 companies, a volunteer along with other Olympians to speak in schools in an effort to fight childhood obesity, a sports reporter, a Pilates instructor, and the inspiration for thehealthystuff.com.

In addition, Julie was the 12-time winner of Cincinnati's annual Thanksgiving Day 10K Race. After her years of participation, Julie decided to give back to her sport by volunteering to help organize the race. Shortly thereafter, the race director stepped down, and Julie, who is predisposed to saying "yes" to opportunities, stepped into the role. Although she says the experience has been a roller coaster of joys and woes, the results speak for themselves. Under her more than a decade of direction, the race has grown to 17,000 runners, is the eighth largest 10K in the country, and has been selected by *Men's Journal* to be one of the top ten Turkey Trots in the country. Julie is still winning the Cincinnati Thanksgiving Day Race and in life, but simply in another capacity. And she has no lack of entries in the gratitude journal she adds to on a daily basis.

For Julie, retirement is the wrong word, and she helps us think not of "withdrawal," but of "opportunity;" not of "departure," but of "fulfillment;" not of "retreat," but of "engagement."

Chapter 2

Who Am I Now?

"You're talking about an identity crisis. Every athlete has to face the same question when they're done: 'Who am I?'"
Troy Vincent

"Most guys don't understand that playing the game is only what you do...it's not who you are."
Deion Sanders

What do these elite athletes have in common, other than they are retired from successful professional careers?

> Quarterback Jim McMahon retired at age 37 from a 14-year NFL career, during which he earned both Rookie of the Year and Comeback Player of the Year honors, was a Pro Bowl selection, and played on two Super Bowl championship teams. This followed a college career at BYU, during which he set 70 NCAA records.
> Forward Antoine Walker retired at age 32 from a 12-year NBA career. He was an overall sixth draft pick of the Boston Celtics, made the All-Rookie First Team in a year in which he lead the Celtics in scoring, played on one NBA championship team, and was a three-time All-Star.
> Race car driver Dale Jarrett retired at age 52 from a 24-year NASCAR career, in which he won 32 races and was the 1999 Winston Cup Series Champion. In 2014, he was inducted into the NASCAR Hall of Fame.
> Pitcher Hideki Irabu retired at age 31 from a five-year MLB career, which followed eight years in Japanese professional baseball. Irabu

sported a 98 mile per hour fastball and averaged over seven strike outs per nine innings.

> British light welterweight, Ricky Hatton, retired at age 32 from a 14-year professional boxing career, in which he won 45 of his 48 bouts, 32 by knockout. He had held seven British amateur titles and several professional championships.

What they have in common is having significantly struggled in their transition into and through retirement.

> McMahon has suffered from both depression and early onset dementia. Although doctors have helped him through the toughest of times, McMahon has said, "I am glad I don't have any weapons in my house or else I am pretty sure I wouldn't be here." McMahon believes the issues derive from the physical punishment he absorbed playing football.

> Despite making tens of millions of dollars during his career, Walker declared bankruptcy within two years of his retirement. He speaks openly about his issues, "When you come into the league when you're 19 years old, you're not really trained...on business decisions and how to manage your money."

> Although he retired at an older age than the vast majority of elite athletes, Jarrett found it a very low period in his life, "There were times I was so depressed after I retired that I didn't know what it would take to get out of that. I don't have any doubt that's a definite factor in my going through a divorce."

> Nine years after retiring from Major League Baseball and two months after he and his wife separated, Irabu hanged himself. He never settled into a meaningful retirement and had battled both alcohol abuse and aggression issues.

> Hatton announced his retirement two years after being knocked out by Manny Pacquiao in 2009, but he had not stepped into a ring in the interim. He says, "I was crying...and contemplating suicide...I was going deeper and deeper into depression." He had also added drugs and alcohol to his mix of issues.

Certainly these are among the extreme cases, but sadly, situations like these are not all that rare among elite athletes when their careers end. Even when retired athletes successfully redefine themselves and create fulfilling post-career lives, many still profess that the transition was difficult. Recall Julie Isphording's insight that between one door closing and another opening, it is frequently "hell in the hallway."

Older non-athletes who retire from careers to which they have been deeply committed can encounter similarly serious challenges. The fastest growing divorce rate among any segment of society is couples over the age of 55. It is estimated that about 2,000,000 retired Boomers exhibit symptoms of depression during any given year. The segment of society with the highest suicide rate are men over the age of 70. Again, these may be the most extreme of cases, but the risks are there.

The retirement challenges that lie ahead for most may not be as severe as those experienced by McMahon, Walker, Jarrett, Irabu, or Hatton or by the older generation in the statistics noted above. But it's important when developing a winning retirement game plan to recognize the reality that challenges do exist.

A Vision

Although Baseball Hall-of-Famer John McGraw went on to an exceptional managerial career, when he retired from his 16-year playing career (batting average .334; OBP .466) in 1906 at age 33, he lamented, "If the best thing has already happened, what's next?"

Despite, McGraw's sentiments and the risks highlighted above, it is not my intent to create a fear of retirement. In fact, before we dig more deeply into the challenges, let's look at a compelling vision of what retirement can and should be. As you do, think about the key words in McGraw's statement, "What's next?" Try this on for size.

Envision a time in your life when you are full of energy and contented at the same time. Your life is filled with close relationships with family and friends; you are contributing your time and resources to helping others; your days, weeks, months, and years are filled with activities that you love, that help you grow, and that are just plain fun. You awaken each day with a positive attitude about life and are clear about your life's purpose. You have the resources and general well-being to live a life that makes you happy and can foresee living it well into your future. You take advantage of new-found opportunities, and you deal with life's inevitable setbacks, because you are resilient and have a game plan that helps guide you through them.

Whether you are already retired or yet to do so, whether you are an elite athlete or an older non-athlete in an all-consuming career, this is a vision you can realistically create, plan for, and live.

Losses

Many of the challenges of transitioning into and through retirement derive from what you have left behind as you leave your primary career. When you are playing your sport or working at your profession, there are things that come your way as part of just showing up each day.

Think about it—here are some things your sport or profession provide. The role you perform affords you a personal identity. You receive recognition and adulation from others. You have a built-in structure and a schedule of things to do. You have close relationships with teammates, colleagues, and others associated with your work. You have no lack of triggers for an adrenaline rush. Your pay provides you with a basis for financial security. If you are an elite athlete, fitness is part of what you do. You are intellectually stimulated by those around you and the work that you do. And you are surrounded by coaches, bosses, peers, and others who help you hold yourself accountable to your goals and for your actions.

In thinking about what your career provides you but that you no longer have the day after your retire, and as you develop your retirement game plan through the remainder of the book, keep these three key words in mind, "inevitable," "normal," and "control."

It is "inevitable," when you retire, that you will lose these important life factors that had been provided to you by your work. The emotional turmoil you will experience as a result of the losses is "normal." It is within your "control" to identify and engage in activities that will serve to replace what you have lost.

If you are already retired, these losses may already be affecting you. If you are still playing/working, you may have never considered these risks. In either case, it is important to better understand each one of the losses you may encounter. The order in which they are discussed is not intended to indicate priority or severity, as these will affect each of us differently. They are numbered for reference only.

1. Loss: Personal Identity; Who am I now?
2. Loss: Recognition/Adulation; How will I deal with leaving the limelight?
3. Loss: Structure and Things to Do; What should I do now?
4. Loss: Relationships; Who will be my new circle of meaningful friends? What are my new family dynamics?
5. Loss: Financial Security; How will I be and feel financially secure?
6. Loss: Fitness; How will I stay fit?
7. Loss: Accountability Structure; How will I hold myself accountable?

Be assured that we will address each of these issues as the book unfolds. But it is critical to understand what the challenges may look like in order to deal with them.

Loss #1
Personal Identity; Who am I now?

Bob Tewksbury, retired major league pitcher and former director of player development for the Major League Baseball Players Association, has a Master's degree in sports psychology and counseling from Boston University. Tewksbury has said, "The biggest single thing in career transition is identifying who athletes are when they are no longer an athlete."

In his memoir, *Eleven Rings: The Soul of Success*, retired NBA player and coach, Phil Jackson, reflects on the time when he had just finished his NBA playing career at age 35.

Somewhere on the outskirts of Piscataway, I found myself having an imaginary conversation with my father, who had died a few months earlier.

"What am I going to do, Dad?" I said. "Is the rest of my life going to be total drudgery, just going through the motions?"

Pause.

"How can anything else ever be as meaningful to me as playing basketball? Where am I going to find my new purpose in life?"

It would take several years to find the answer.

Whether consciously or subconsciously, doesn't every retiring professional athlete have that conversation with him or herself? And doesn't everyone who is retiring, regardless of career or age, have a comparable cause and pause for self-reflection? Finding a post-career life purpose can be an especially thorny matter for those who have put their heart and soul into their work and must then make the transition to a life purpose that is no longer defined by that work.

The International Olympic Committee published a document entitled "Athletic Identity and Sport Transition" with their stated intent to "...underline the importance of this issue in the light of career transitions, and to show how it can influence...the quality of athlete's retirement."

In the publication, the IOC answers the question, "Why is it important to examine athletic identity in light of my career after retirement?" In part they answer, "Be aware that a transition out of sport implies identity change: when putting an end to their sporting career, athletes lose an important part of themselves...the loss of their sporting role dramatically increases the intensity of the identity crisis."

This is clearly not an issue for athletes alone. Anyone who has been passionate about his or her career can struggle when leaving that phase of life. Tom Terrien is the cofounder of the National Association of Retired Physicians. On the association's web site, Terrien reports, "My father,

Christopher Terrien, M.D., enjoyed a long and successful career as one of the first Cardiologists of note in the state of Vermont. He was a practicing physician in the State for 40 years and was chief of medical staff at the teaching hospital in Burlington...After decades of playing a role, of healing people, of making serious decisions every day, he was suddenly separated from all of that. I saw firsthand what happens when a vital, dedicated member of the medical community is deprived of the opportunity to contribute...this was a loss of purpose for my father."

Scott Farley played for the NFL New England Patriots and Carolina Panthers before retiring in 2006, when he tore his hamstring all the way off the bone. After 18 months of surgery and rehab, he attempted a comeback with the Rhein Fire of NFL Europa. Farley said, "There's a loss of identity after you're done playing sports, because you obviously identify yourself as a competitor, as an athlete, someone who thrives on the competitive and euphoric nature that comes with the sport you're playing."

The roles we play can reflect our life purpose, but the roles are not the purpose itself. Are you a second baseman, a project manager, a snowboarder, a Vice President of Marketing, a defenseman, a special education teacher, a tight end, a literary agent? Each is a role, not a life purpose.

That being said, replacing your career role with a different one in retirement, can be helpful. Will you be a volunteer, a coach, an entrepreneur? Will you be a nonprofit board member, consultant, commentator? Will you be an author, part-time community college teacher? Will you find a full-blown second/encore career?

It is a myth that retirement means not working. This is especially true for elite athletes, who retire at such a young age.

The International Olympic Committee is explicit about this issue as well and is attempting to address it with their "IOC Athlete Career Programme." The IOC states, "Many athletes retire from elite sport without acquiring an education, training or life skills. This typically leaves them unprepared for the transition to work from their sporting career...with no tangible means of entry into an alternative occupation or profession."

Leigh Steinberg, the prominent sports agent, thinks enough of this issue to offer the athletes he represents a program called "Second Career." The program is designed to help clients create a foundation to build on after sport careers are over.

The magic happens when whatever role you choose in retirement is aligned with what you determine is your identity, your life purpose. Figuring out how to replace the loss of the identity provided by the role you play in your primary career will be part of the challenge of your retirement transition.

Loss #2
Recognition/Adulation: How will I deal with leaving the limelight?

This loss is a corollary to Loss #1, "Who am I now?" And it is the basis of the title of this book, *After the Cheering Stops*.

In a 2012 op-ed piece for the *Chicago Sun-Times*, Bears wide receiver Brandon Marshall wrote, "As athletes, we go through life getting praised and worshipped and making a lot of money. Our worlds and everything in them—spouses, kids, family, religion and friends—revolve around us. We create a world where our sport is our life and makes us who we are. When the game is taken away from us or when we stop playing, the shock of not hearing the praise or receiving the big bucks often turns out to be devastating."

In his book, *Days of Grace*, tennis legend Arthur Ashe wrote, "Most athletes, no matter how intelligent they may be, are almost totally unprepared to retire, as they are forced to do, while they are in their physical prime. I was at least as cautious and reflective as the next professional, but I know that I was not adequately prepared to take the step. Remove the glitter and glamour of the tennis world, I wondered, the endless stroking of the ego, the copious episodes of pampering and privilege, and where would I be? Would I be haunting bars and picking up women, or loafing in my 'den,' swilling beer and playing video cassettes of the highlights of my career over and over to my 'buddies,' or to myself?"

Since all-pro linebacker Junior Seau committed suicide three years after retiring from the game, much has been written about chronic traumatic encephalopathy, the degenerative brain disease that may have been caused by the multitude of blows to the head Seau experienced during his football career. But his former San Diego Charger teammate, Miles McPherson, reflected on something else Seau may have been dealing with, "When you grow up an athlete and you live in a world that praises you all the time as you go from high school to college, college to the pros, the decibel volume, the number of people, the frequency of praise that comes your way, increases. By the time you get to play 20 years in the NFL, in 12 consecutive Pro Bowls, and all that comes with that, you're living in fantasyland. All that one day stops. But your body, mind and heart are conditioned to such a high level of excitement, adrenaline rush, challenge, and then you're like taken off the drug, cold turkey. A lot of guys, women as well, celebrities, who live in a bubble, have a hard time living with normal life. Unless they can emotionally and spiritually handle the letdown and transition to something that will satisfy them, even though it will never bring the adrenaline rush their career did, they're somewhat at a loss."

Have non-athletes, perhaps other than entertainers, politicians, and a few other exceptions, experienced the exhilaration of being cheered by thousands of people, of being seen on TV by millions, of seeing their name in headlines and their performance on highlight reels, of being constantly sought after for autographs, interviews, and selfies? No. But non-athletes do have careers that bring the consistent recognition of subordinates (executives, business founders and owners, military officers), parents and students (teachers), patients (physicians), clients (attorneys), audiences (public speakers), customers (many professions).

In the Arthur Ashe and Miles McPherson quotations, you see phrases like "stroking of the ego," "pampering and privilege," "praise," and "adrenaline rush." Most careers, both athletic and not, provide the brightness of the limelight—then, "All that one day stops."

At the time Brad Daugherty retired from the Cleveland Cavaliers at age 30 because of an injury, he was their all-time leader in career points. The joy of golfing, hunting, and fishing wore off quickly. It's called "hedonic adaptation"—look it up. Several years into his retirement, Daugherty said, "If I could go play today, right now, you could keep the damn money. I want to feel the competition again. I'd play for free if you'd just let me go out and feel that desire to win again. Nothing replaces it."

Whether it is the limelight and all that comes with it or just the high from the competition, retirees can frequently struggle to replace the "stroking of the ego" and the "adrenaline rush."

Any Suicide…is problematic

Mentioning Junior Seau prompts me to address a difficult subject in the context of this chapter, but one that needs to be on the table.

➤ The Society of Baseball Research (SABR) has determined that of the approximately 13,000 professional players in the game's history, 98 have committed suicide. That is a rate of 754 per 100,000. The global and U.S. rates for suicides are 16 and 11 per 100,000, respectively.

➤ More than 150 cricket players have committed suicide, including the popular Yorkshire wicketkeeper, David Bairstow. Reports indicate that at age 46, having been retired for eight years, he was suffering from depression, was facing a drunk-driving charge, and was in pain from career injuries. Depression can be a challenge for athletes and older retirees alike—while the statistics are not fully reliable, it is clear that symptoms are not uncommon.

➤ There has been a rash of suicides of NHL retired and current players, most who have been suffering from symptoms of depression— including three in a four-month span in 2011. The most recent was former NHL enforcer Todd Ewen, age 49.

➤ Clarke Carlisle retired from English football after the 2013 season, having played defender for his 18-year career, during which he was honored by his fellow sportsmen by being chosen as chairman of the Professional Footballers Association. An 18-month bout with depression followed his retirement, and in 2015, he spent six weeks in the hospital after being hit by a truck, only to admit, "I stepped in front of a lorry because I wanted to die."

There are also studies to show that athletes are no more likely to commit suicide than their non-sports-career counterparts. That being said, whether the stats are comparable or not, any suicide, especially one that is anecdotally connected to sports careers or retiring from them, is problematic.

And did you know that the segment of society with the highest suicide rate are men over the age of 70? Some speculate that this is a function of a loss of meaning in their lives. Others believe that men are more poorly equipped to deal with issues, being less resilient when they lose the ability to control the conditions of their lives. Whatever the comparative statistics or the root cause, it is clear that suicide is an issue across generations of retirees.

Loss #3
Structure and Things to Do:
What should I do now?

When Pete Sampras, winner of 14 tennis Grand Slam titles and holder of the year-end Number 1 world ranking for six consecutive years, was interviewed a full decade after he retired, he said, "Retirement is a work in progress. I try to figure out my day, and what I know about myself is that I need structure."

A 2012 on-line ESPN article, "Life after NFL a Challenge for Many," included what former NFL quarterback Trent Green said about his retirement, "The hardest part is your daily routine. For 15 years, I knew exactly what I was doing in March, June, and September because there was a schedule. When you take that away, you suddenly have a lot more time on your hands. I've been out of the game since 2008, and I still have a tough time with it. I find myself thinking, 'What's my motivation today?'"

Despite articulating the issue very well, Green may have understated it. He referred to his 15 years in the NFL but did not mention the four years he played for Indiana University or his four years at Vianney High School in a St. Louis suburb before that. Nor did he talk about youth football. And he didn't say that the schedule to which he refers included rigorous practices, film sessions, strength training, travel itineraries, strategy meetings, pre-game preparation and warm-ups, and the games themselves. And he did not mention that virtually all of that scheduling was dictated by someone else.

I've had the occasion in retirement life planning workshops to ask thousands of Baby Boomers to identify what their work careers provide for them that they will need to replace in retirement. Invariably one of the first things shouted out is "structure."

The work years for non-athletes are structured by projects, appointments, meetings, travel schedules, class schedules, customer calls, business plans and cycles, and on and on. And much of that scheduling is dictated by others. Discretionary time is a rare luxury.

I frequently hear from those close to the retiree, "I'm really worried about him (or her). He has no hobbies. His whole life has been his work. He'll have nothing to do."

And if the person telling me this is a wife, she'll quickly follow with something like, "And he's going to drive me nuts."

In his memoir, *The Outsider*, Jimmy Connors wrote about his transition from tennis tour to home life with his wife, Patti, and their children. "In the days, weeks, and months after I finally accepted the reality that I was off the tour for good, I went through a really rough time, tougher than I thought it would be. For so many years, time had been measured by events and tournaments, not days and months. January was the Masters, May was Roland Garros, June was Wimbledon, September the US Open. That's not a normal way to live, and when that's gone, it's unsettling. Tennis had been my life...Now it was gone. Just like that."

In retirement, your schedule, your structure is your own. You are your own coach, your own boss. This freedom is an opportunity, but it is also a challenge.

The late Oail Andrew "Bum" Phillips, who coached football at the high school, college, and professional levels, retired at age 62. Phillips hit the nail on the head for any retiree who has not developed a robust game plan. He was asked about his retirement and responded, "I ain't doing a damn thing, and I don't start until noon."

Loss #4
Relationships: Who will be my
new circle of friends?

Take 13 minutes and watch Robert Waldinger's Ted-talk at ted.com. He reports on the results of the longest (75 year) study ever conducted to understand the factors that most likely result in a good and happy life. He emphasizes that the results of the study reveal that the depth of our personal relationships has a meaningful impact on both longevity and quality of life.

Yet for many, work colleagues and teammates turn out to really be only situational acquaintances and not really the deep personal friends that can make that meaningful long-lasting difference in our lives.

A much-respected colleague had one of the largest retirement parties our company had ever seen. Several hundred gathered, including the then-current and two previous CEO's. About a year after Steve retired, he was asked if there had been any surprises in his new life. Steve responded, "It turned out that all of the friends I thought I had at work really weren't. In this past year, only three former colleagues have called me to see how I was doing."

Although Steve is now living a full and fulfilling retirement, in large part because of a deep passion for and commitment to the Boy Scouts, he experienced symptoms of depression in those early years. Steve is not unusual, and it took him some time to develop and nurture friendships outside the workplace.

There may be no more intense workplace relationships than those built among sports teammates in locker rooms, in dugouts, on benches, and on the field, court, course, or pitch. Not only do athletic teammates work together, but during a season, road trips have them living together. Hopefully what Jesse Owens, the celebrated and historic four-gold-medal winner in the 1936 Berlin Olympics, said is correct for you, "Friendships born on the field of athletic strife are the real gold of competition. Awards become corroded, friends gather no dust."

But Owens's insight is too frequently not the case. John Michels retired from a career as an offensive lineman for the Green Bay Packers at the age of

26, following his sixth knee surgery. He describes the issue of friendships, "Once you retire, the silence is deafening. No one calls, not even your former teammates. It's like you've been kicked out of the locker room."

It's not just about leaving the locker room or team plane or practice field. The elite level of sports is a transient business. Teammates today are not always teammates tomorrow.

In 2011, Michael Wilczynski studied the transient nature of professional basketball careers. He found that NBA players spend, on average, only 2.2 seasons with any one team and play for an average of 2.5 teams during their short careers.

Certainly, there are exceptions. For example, Jerry West played his 14-year career with the Lakers; John Havlicek played 16 years with the Celtics, Reggie Miller 18 years with the Pacers, Kobe Bryant 20 years with the Lakers. There are also players who have played for well more than their fair share of teams. Consider Chucky "Wild Thing" Brown's 12-year career in which he played for 12 different teams and several of those more than once.

Major League Baseball mirrors the NBA. Kevin Pauga's study found that the average major league player will play for 2.2 teams.

The transient nature of a career is not limited to elite athletes. In my 33-year career, I worked in three different business disciplines, Manufacturing, Research & Development, and Quality Assurance. I spent eight years at a manufacturing plant in Northeast Pennsylvania and the remainder of my career in Cincinnati, and I was offered an assignment in Germany, which I chose not to pursue. Most of my colleagues moved much more frequently than did I.

Bosses, subordinates, and project teammates changed frequently. During my last job assignment, my team was spread around the world. Yes, there were some people at work that I considered friends. And yes, a couple of them have continued to be friends in retirement. But the vast majority of people I worked with were not close friends.

Everyone approaching retirement should be thinking about whether they have deep personal relationships that will carry over and contribute to a fulfilling post-career life. Or are your professional relationships merely fleeting, only relevant in the workplace or "on the field of athletic strife?"

Loss #4 (Part B)
Relationships: What are my new family dynamics?

Retirement also brings a change to the relationships with family members at home.

As noted earlier, the segment of society with the fastest growing divorce rate is couples over the age of 55. A retired couple came up to me after a retirement life-planning workshop. The husband said, "We're okay now, but it has taken awhile. When we retired, we hadn't acknowledged that we had relationship issues. Suddenly we were together all day every day and had to deal with the problems. Before that, we addressed them by going to work and ignoring them."

Here's an extreme example I came across. Bob was offered a retirement package by his employer and jumped at the chance to live out his lifelong dream, sailing around the world. At first blush, that sounds exciting and an opportunity to pursue his passion. The problems arose because of how he approached it.

Bob had never before shared his sailing dream with his wife, Linda. The day he was offered the package, he came home and told her he was retiring and they would be sailing around the world. When Linda was hesitant, Bob said she could either come with him or he would be leaving without her. She relented, but you can see where this was heading.

He researched boats and decided what he wanted to buy and enrolled both of them in sailing courses. Then, for the first time, he approached a financial advisor and described what he wanted to do, including withdrawing the high cost of the boat from his retirement funds, with all of the negative implications. Against advice, Bob forged ahead.

They were on the boat for only a couple of months when she decided it had been a bad idea from the beginning. She left, flew home, and filed for divorce.

Extreme? Yes. Instructive? Also yes!

Here's an experience with interviews with two different Baby Boomer couples the same week, each with the husband having recently retired and each interview the same, almost word-for-word. First question went to the husband without the wife in the room, "How is your new retirement experience going?"

"It's going great. I have lots of free time. Do you know what I did last week? I reorganized the kitchen cabinets."

You'll not be surprised about what happened next. To the wife, without the husband in the room, "How is your husband's retirement going?"

"You've got to be kidding. Do you know what he did? He rearranged my cabinets. I can't wait until he finds another job or something else to do—outside the house."

This sounds very similar to what Jimmy Connors wrote, "'Jeez, Jimmy,' Patti would say, 'don't you have somewhere to go?'"

Some studies report the divorce rate of retired athletes to be much greater than the general population. Others say there's no difference. Regardless of which is true, the challenge is the same—how to successfully make the transition to a new lifestyle in which the family may be together much more of the time.

The challenge is magnified when you consider that a very small percentage of couples have discussed their retirement plans sufficiently to be sure they are aligned. Some individuals have actually told us that they don't talk about it with their partner at all, because they know they don't agree on some big decisions, and instead of working through them, they choose not to confront their differences.

Just as the relationships of your teammates and work colleagues will be a loss when you retire, so will you experience a loss if your retirement contributes to a divorce.

There are other changes in family dynamics. Because of their age, retiring elite athletes may also be dealing with building new relationships with children. Doug Glanville played nine major league seasons, mostly with the Phillies, before retiring in 2004. He became a baseball analyst for ESPN and ESPN.com as well as an author. But perhaps most importantly, he is a father. Glanville wrote, "Throughout my career, I faced quite a few Hall of Famers. Maddux, Glavine, Johnson. They are nowhere near as tough as running a household full of kids 24-7." When he wrote this, Glanville had three children under the age of four.

It is clear that he is a caring and dedicated father with a great perspective on the family dynamics of a young retired athlete, or any young parent. These are but a few of Glanville's truisms of parenthood for the retired athlete:

> ➤ *"No child has to go to the bathroom until you have dressed them all in their snowsuits and then buckled them into their car seats and are about to pull out of the school parking lot."*
> ➤ *"Baby monitors were invented by something evil: Someone went out and decided that you need to watch and listen to your children 29 hours a day, nine days a week..."*
> ➤ *"You probably need a handyman living in your basement."*

By contrast, for older retirees, their children may be grown, perhaps with families of their own. Yet it is also true that the trend of adult children living with their parents has been increasing since 2005, at which time the statistic was 27%. As of this writing, it is just under 32%.

Having them living at home is not the only effect that adult children can have on older retirees. About 35% of grandparents expect to provide some support for their grandchildren, including direct financial support and helping pay for housing, education, and health care. This is not necessarily a bad thing, but the circumstances should be factored into both financial and life planning for retirement.

AARP reports that more than 5.8 million children are living in their grandparents' home for a number of reasons. A University of Chicago study found that more than 60% of grandparents provided at least 50 hours a year of care for grandchildren for at least one year. A MetLife analysis found similar results and also reported that about 60% of grandparents have at least one grandchild within 50 miles, and 74% of those grandparents baby sit or provide care weekly.

"Boomerang children" are not the only family dynamic for Boomers. A separate MetLife study found that 10 million over the age of 50 care for their aging parents, a number that has more than tripled over the past 15 years. Providing this care has both emotional and financial implications.

Although the reasons may be different across the generations, retirement can be a time of new and stressful family dynamics.

Janna LaCock
Ex-Wife of Pete LaCock,
Major League Baseball "Stress"

Janna LaCock is the Executive Director of the Mid-America Chapter of the Leukemia and Lymphoma Society. She manages a large staff, a significant budget, and a complex and meaningful program. Her organization's work helps blood cancer patients cope with and fight their disease, and her personal contribution to this effort helps define her.

But Janna has another identity—she is the ex-wife of Pete LaCock, who played for the Cubs and the Royals during his nine-year MLB career, after which he played briefly in Japan, before retiring after the 1981 season. Besides playing professional baseball, Pete has two other claims to fame. He is the son of TV personality Peter Marshall, who among other things, was the long-time host of "The Hollywood Squares." And Pete hit his only career MLB grand-slam off of Bob Gibson in what would be Gibson's final major league appearance in September 1975.

As an aside, more than a decade later, Gibson and LaCock were both playing in an old-timer's game. Gibson, facing LaCock for the first time since the grand slam, hit Pete in the back with a fastball. Payback.

Janna reports that when Pete retired, he struggled with a wide range of issues that put a strain on their relationship, which she had anticipated, having watched other players and spouses go through the transition. There was financial stress, both in the management of spending and in her lack of confidence in the financial advice they were being given. There was proximity stress. Janna, like other spouses, had grown strong and independent over the years, having managed the household and family in the frequent absence of the player. Pete was now home all of the time.

And perhaps most of all, Janna felt the stress that Pete was feeling as he searched desperately to redefine himself, find meaning and structure in this new phase of his life, and find something to do that, in Janna's words, "he could be proud of." They were struggling with the issue, when Pete finally put his words to it, "If I'm not a baseball player, then what am I?"

Janna built a new and fulfilling life—Pete had a more difficult time doing so.

Loss #5
Financial Security: How will I be and feel financially secure?

There are two issues wrapped up in the real and/or perceived loss of financial security when one retires. The first is that the paychecks stop. Not only is salary no longer coming in, but the secure feeling of knowing that there is regular income from the job is gone.

We interviewed a retired corporate executive, who by any measure was financially well off. She had a significant portfolio, was receiving expert financial advice, and had begun what was on the verge of becoming a very successful retirement business. Yet she said, "It took me almost 18 months and a lot of support from friends to get comfortable with the fact that the corporate paycheck was no longer coming in monthly."

Was she financially OK? Yes. Did she feel financially secure? No.

The second issue of loss does, in fact, have to do with the income no longer flowing, which coupled with overspending, can be disastrous. Another extreme example makes the point, but the concept applies at any level of overspending. A recently retired couple I learned about were introduced to some fellow golf lovers, who lived and played at a local country club. Liking the feeling and wanting to fit in, they grossly overextended themselves when they bought a house on the golf course and joined the club. The cost of the house and furnishing it, as well as continuing to keep up with the lifestyles of other members, resulted in a complete depletion of their savings. The lure of instant gratification led to a lack of spending discipline and negatively affected the remainder of their retirement.

Former Baltimore Orioles and California Angel, six-time All-Star, and four-time Gold Glove winner, Bobby Grich, has said, "Players are not trained in wealth management, and that world can be totally intimidating, as I know from personal experience."

The oft-cited 2009 *Sports Illustrated* study noted:

> ➤ Within two years of retirement, 78% of former NFL players have gone bankrupt or are experiencing financial stress because of joblessness or divorce.
> ➤ An estimated 60% of former NBA players are broke within five years of retirement.
> ➤ Many former MLB players reported being broke and a number of active players were asking for advances on their salaries to cover debts.

More recently reported, 60% of English Premier League footballers (soccer players) have declared bankruptcy.

The reasons for the financial woes cited in the *Sports Illustrated* article and echoed in the ESPN "30 for 30" documentary, *Broke*, are numerous: being targets for get-rich-quick schemes without the sophistication, time, or inclination to sort out good from bad; family matters including divorce and child support; the financial drain of and misplaced trust in family, friends, the entourage, and even supposedly trusted advisors; and just plain extravagant overspending.

Financial security is not about the size of the nest egg. Rather, it is about understanding what your available resources are, understanding the cost (budget) of your lifestyle, and then matching the lifestyle to the resources. The challenge is in both the understanding and the matching.

Another challenge is to understand and believe that it is a myth of retirement and of life in general that money equals happiness. The research is consistent—only a small portion of our happiness comes from material things. "Sure," you might say, "give me that burden, and I'll prove you wrong." But talk to lottery winners and others with large nest eggs. They may be happy, but it's not the finances that are driving that happiness.

That being said, you do need to attend to your finances as one of the things to pay attention to—just not the only thing. Reggie Wilkes, former

Eagles and Falcons linebacker and now a Senior Financial Advisor at Merrill Lynch, shares with his elite athlete clients that they should have a "financial game plan" just as they have a sports game plan.

Great advice! "Game plan." Sound familiar?

Loss #6
Fitness: How will I stay fit?

A retiring professional soccer player is likely to be about 30 years old and coming off one of his or her typical seasons, 46 weeks of conditioning and strength training six days a week and a full schedule of practices and games. A retiring 60-year old, coming off one of his or her typical years, has spent most of the day sitting at a desk, sitting while grading papers or preparing for tomorrow's classes or meetings or presentations, sitting in airports or on planes traveling to where the business needs are, and taking little time for personal fitness.

When I retired, I lost 15 pounds and two inches off my waist in the first six months with no special diet. I simply shifted from business dinners, airplane food, and eating lunch at my desk to more nutritional normal amounts at normal times. And I was able to get to the gym on a regular basis. That being said, despite concerted efforts, it is unrealistic to believe that my fitness level will be anywhere near the fitness level of my elite athlete retiree counterpart.

Shannon Miller, America's most decorated gymnast and two-time inductee into the United States Olympic Hall of Fame, had the opposite problem. "I didn't know how to be a regular person. Prior to retiring, I was eating six full meals a day, because I was burning it all off at the gym. Once retired, I initially watched a lot of TV, gaining four dress sizes on my five foot frame. It was very disheartening, but it helped me realize I had to find my next passion in life."

Miller did just that. She earned two undergraduate degrees from the University of Houston and her law degree from Boston College. She is in shape, President of Shannon Miller Lifestyle, which "promotes a healthy and balanced lifestyle," the mother of two, and cancer free after a diagnosis of and the treatment for a rare form of ovarian cancer.

Certainly, professional football is a more violent sport than others, but this extreme example helps make the point about injury and wear and tear effects on the retired athlete. A 2010 study was conducted among 644 NFL players who retired between 1979 and 2006 and played for an average of eight years. The investigation found that these former players were using painkilling opioid drugs at a rate three times that of the general population, 93% reporting pain and 81% perceiving their pain to be moderate to severe.

Jim Otto, Pro Football Hall of Fame center for the Oakland Raiders, never missed a game, playing 308 consecutively, including regular season, post season, and 12 All-Star games, despite constantly fending off injuries. Over the course of his career and in retirement, he has had over 70 surgeries, several of which led to life-threatening infections, and one which forced the amputation of his right leg. A high-tech prosthetic and a great sense of humor have gotten him through, but Otto certainly paid the price for his professional career.

Extreme examples exist in other sports as well. For example, Kevin Pearce, among the top few snowboarding professionals in the world, suffered a traumatic brain injury while training for the Olympics in Park City, forcing him to retire in 2009 at age 22. Kevin's recovery has been remarkable, and he has dedicated himself, through his "Love Your Brain Foundation," to help others with brain injuries.

Although most elite athletes deal with lesser issues, the wear and tear on their bodies can be debilitating nevertheless. Mike Piazza, baseball Hall-of-Famer and 12-time MLB All-Star catcher, who squatted behind the plate in well over 1500 games, said, "Everyone is asking, 'How are your knees? How are your knees?' And I'm thinking, 'My back! I can't even tie my shoes sometimes in the morning!'"

Research reported in the *British Journal of Sports Medicine* found that among 284 retired soccer players studied, nearly half had arthritis in a weight-bearing joint while never having sustained a serious injury in that joint. Hip problems occurred ten times more frequently in the former athletes than in a control group that had never played professional sports, and six of the players had already had hip replacements before or while in their 40s.

Are retired Boomers pain free and all in excellent general health? Of course not. Just sit around a table with a group in their 60s, and before the discussion ends, you will have heard about everyone's aches, pains, illnesses, surgeries, meds, and doctors. Do you want to see the scars from my two hip replacements? By the way, once I worked through the rehab, I'm pain free, off of anti-inflammatories for the first time in 15 years, and still playing baseball in my 70s—thanks for asking.

Age has its own wear and tear effect, but there are two differences. The retired athlete is more likely to develop debilitating issues and he or she will be dealing with the problems over a much longer timeframe. Then they can look forward to the issues being exacerbated as age begins to play a role for them as well.

Loss of a rigorous and well-monitored fitness regimen. Loss of body functionality from wear and tear and injury. Loss of body functionality from age. All of these can affect retirement.

Loss #7
Accountability Structure: How will I hold myself accountable?

At work, non-athletes are accountable to the boss, to customers, to colleagues, and to the business itself. Elite athletes are accountable to the general manager, to the coach, to fans, to teammates, and to the game itself.

Salespeople are measured by dollars of sales; teachers by results of their students on standardized tests; engineers by the reliability of equipment designs; CEOs by the Profit & Loss statement. Elite athletes are measured more than virtually any other segment of society. What is your ERA, YAC, RBI, PPG, OPS, W-L, WHIP, fairways hit, break point %, split times, and on and on? There are organizations and commentators dedicated to dissecting every possible angle of athletic performance.

To get a sense of how extensively athletes are measured, I looked up Derek Jeter's career statistics. The first chart showed his "Standard Batting" stats by year of his career. There were 30 columns of stats labeled across the top of the chart. Scrolling down on that page I found three other charts, displaying his "Postseason Batting," "Player Value—Batters," and "Fielding," each by year with its volume of columns.

The page also had a tab labeled, "More Stats." Click. On the new page were charts for "Advanced Batting," "All-Star Batting," "Ratio Batting," "Win Probability," "Baserunning & Misc. Stats," "Situational Batting," "Pitch Summary—Batting," "Cumulative Batting," "Neutralized Batting," each by year and with multiple columns. And there were even more stats that were not in the same chart form—"Hall of Fame Statistics," "Similarity Scores," and something called "Appearances on Leader Boards, Awards, and Honors," for which Jeter appropriately had substantial entries.

I've been an engaged baseball fan, player, and coach for over six decades, and I must admit, I didn't recognize many of the stats by which Jeter was measured.

Before retirement, regardless of your profession, you are accountable and measured. When you retire, who will help you hold yourself accountable? How will you know how you are doing? Perhaps this lack of oversight is a degree of freedom you will enjoy. But it might also bring uncertainty. What will be the foundation of your self-esteem in retirement? Will you be able to switch gears and hold yourself accountable to get the things done that will make your life full and fulfilling?

Cody Mivshek was a two-time All-State 6-foot-2 guard for the Fossil Ridge High School basketball team in Fort Collins, Colorado and went on to play college ball for the University of Portland and Claremont McKenna College. In his 2015 article, "I'm a Retired College Athlete—Now What Do I Train For," Mivshek wrote, "Leaving college also means losing that level of accountability that is hard to replace...new activities will hinge on the people I surround myself with. The more party animals and couch potatoes I hang out with, the more I'll be just like them. Finding those friends or significant others that can help push you...is important."

We need to be accountable for not overspending, for staying fit, for connecting with family and friends, for giving back to others, for stretching ourselves to learn new things, for developing and maintaining a positive attitude, for so many things. But the coaches are gone. The bosses are gone. The stats are gone. How will we know we are winning *After the Cheering Stops*? And who will help?

Ken Holtzman
Major League Pitcher
"miss...the intense high level competition"

If you want to ask someone a baseball trivia question that they are unlikely to answer correctly, try this, "Who is the winningest Jewish pitcher in major league baseball history?"

Most people will sport a knowing smile, ready to impress you, thinking that the question is more about knowing which pitchers were Jewish. Then they'll say, "Sandy Koufax."

Return the knowing smile and say, "Nope—Ken Holtzman."

Holtzman won 174, while Koufax won "only" 165. Of course, Koufax is in the Hall of Fame after compiling an injury-shortened career record 165-87 with a 2.76 ERA and having won three Cy Young Awards (when there was only one given for all of baseball), and an MVP (finishing second in MVP voting twice).

Holtzman finished his career with a more-than-respectable 174-150 record and 3.49 ERA, during which he threw two major league no-hitters and appeared in two All-Star games. He also had an impressive 6-4, 2.30 ERA postseason career with the Oakland A's in the early 1970s. During that streak, Holtzman batted .308 in his 13 postseason games with a 1.126 OPS, and he holds the major-league career batting records for slugging percentage (0.833), doubles (3), and extra base hits (4) by a pitcher in World Series play.

And yes, Holtzman and Koufax did face each other. In Holtzman's first major league season, his Cubs faced the Dodgers in Koufax's last season—it was September, 1966. The youngster outdueled the veteran, throwing a no-hitter for eight innings on the way to a 2-1 Cubs win. To be clear, although it was Koufax's last year, it was not so because he had lost his effectiveness. In his 1966 season, Koufax was 27-9 with a 1.73 ERA, the Cy Young Award winner and second (to Roberto Clemente) in MVP voting.

Holtzman's baseball career began at seven-years old in Khoury League, the youth baseball program in his native St. Louis, where he dominated and continued to do so through high school, when in 1963, his University City High School team won the Missouri state championship. In that tournament,

Holtzman threw a no-hitter in the semifinals and returned the following day in relief to close out the championship game.

Unlike most elite athletes, Holtzman began thinking about life-after-baseball even before he began his professional career, attributing his foresightedness to the guidance he received from his parents. He negotiated a clause in his contract that would enable him to complete his college education, both in terms of time allowed and allocated salary. Holtzman earned his BA in Business Administration at the University of Illinois during the offseason and was allowed a late start at Cubs' spring training each of his college years.

Holtzman says that when he became the union player representative for the Oakland A's in the early 1970s, he learned "firsthand some of the horror stories of former big league players who were virtually destitute because of low salaries, no educational background, no medical coverage, and other personal circumstances." He vowed not to be like that and started "networking in the business world with people who could help me make the transition when I was ready."

When he retired, he worked at a brokerage house, which along with his deferred baseball salary and major league pension established a sound financial footing. He then returned to college to do something he'd always wanted to do—earn a separate degree in education. Holtzman then leveraged the degree to begin work as the supervisor of health and physical education at the St. Louis Jewish Community Center, both enjoying the work and giving back to the community that had helped him along the way.

Despite his successful transition from his major league baseball career, Holtzman found a couple of things difficult to manage. He reports, "Like most athletes entering retirement, I miss the everyday contact with my teammates and the intense high level competition. There is no substitute in the business world or anywhere else, and it took some years to adjust."

Another part of the transition involved moving from the intensity of the full commitment required to reach and excel at the professional level. Although Holtzman put his commitment into his retirement work, it was not quite the same. He says, "Once you make the decision to turn pro and aspire to reach the big leagues, you must concentrate all of your efforts into self-examination and self-improvement. In my case, it was a matter of constant repetition and dedicated listening to veteran pro players as well as physical practice. It requires constant day-to-day adjustments to keep from being overwhelmed by the best players in the world. Building skills is much more than just mechanics—it includes strategy, concentration, situational awareness, and the ability to critique oneself honestly, as well as taking care of the physical attributes such as eyesight, strength, nutrition, and other vital elements that go into making a high-level athlete."

Chapter 3

It's Inevitable

"I will wonder if I made the wrong decision. I'm sure on Sundays I will say I could be doing that. I should be doing that."
Brett Favre

"The only thing I can do is play baseball. I have to play ball. It's the only thing I know."
Mickey Mantle

On November 24, 1966, Sandy Koufax entered a press conference at the Beverly Wilshire Hotel in Los Angeles. He greeted those assembled, signed some autographs, and proceeded to announce his retirement from the game of baseball at the peak of his 12-year pitching career. These are extracted from his remarks that day.

"I've got a lot of years to live after baseball; I would like to live them with complete use of my body. I don't regret a minute of the last 12 years, but I think I would regret one year that was too many."

"I don't know if cortisone is good for you or not, but when you take a shot after every ballgame, well, that's more than I wanted to do. And then to walk around with a constant upset stomach because of the pills and to be high half the time because of the painkillers during the ballgames, well, I don't want to have to do that."

"The loss of income? Let's put it this way. If there was a man who did not have the use of one of his arms, and you told him it would cost a lot of money and he could buy back that use, I believe he'd give you every dime he had."

Koufax was speaking for himself, but he was also confronting issues facing many elite athletes. He made it clear it was time to move on with life-after-pitching. Although the condition of his arm was the immediate reason for retiring at age 30, leaving his athletic career behind was inevitable—if not in 1966, then one or five or even ten years later. The retirement of every elite athlete is inevitable.

In a 2013 Gallup poll, Baby Boomers were asked when they expected they would retire. About a quarter said they would retire younger than 65; about another quarter said at age 65; and about half said older than 65. Included in that final group were 10% of the Boomers that said they expected never to retire.

It is likely that some number of the never-expect-to-retire group will, in fact, never retire. But it is also likely that health, business conditions, family circumstances, or other reasons will force the issue for most of these career diehards. Said another way, for all intents and purposes, virtually every Boomer, like their elite athlete counterparts, will inevitably retire.

"Inevitability" is the first of three primary phases of retirement. We're about to delve into the phases in more detail, and as we do, I suggest that you focus on two things: 1) which phase you are in, and 2) how each of the phases will affect you, now and into your future.

If you are a vital elite athlete, playing at the college, professional, or Olympic level, why should you be interested in how these phases also relate to the older generation of retirees? Two reasons:

1. Spoiler alert: There is a fourth phase that applies only to you. What is it? It is going through the first three again when you reach the age Baby Boomers are now. That's right. You have the opportunity to retire twice—first from your sports career and again when you retire from what you choose to pursue next.
2. Your parents and others in your life from the older generation can benefit from understanding the phases—and you can help them, just as you will be able to do regarding all of the other concepts in this book that apply to them as well.

Retirement Phase 1
Inevitability

Inevitability is the phase you are in if you are still competing, and it continues through that last game, match, meet, race, or tournament or through that last meeting, business trip, conference call, trial, patient visit, or test to be graded. This phase is the sweet spot to envision, plan for, and practice retirement.

Abby Wambach retired from her storied soccer career having scored 184 international goals for the USA National Team, a world record for both male and female players. She had announced her retirement in October, 2015 and played her final game that December at the age of 35. Despite still being able to compete at the highest level, Wambach stepped down, and declared, "I'm not questioning my decision."

Although she left on her own terms, Wambach's retirement was inevitable. Yes, there are those in every sport who defy the career age norms. But even for those rare athletes, retirement is inescapable.

> ➤ Al Oerter, four-time Olympic Champion in the discus throw; retired initially at age 32 after the 1968 Mexico City Summer Games. In a comeback attempt at age 44, Oerter barely missed qualifying for the 1980 Games by finishing fourth.
> ➤ George Blanda, NFL quarterback and placekicker, who was selected as the league MVP in 1970 at age 43, retired after the 1975 season.
> ➤ Satchel Paige made his MLB pitching debut in 1948 for the Cleveland Indians at age 42, after a legendary Negro Leagues career. He later pitched three scoreless innings for the Kansas City Athletics in 1965 at age 59. When it was announced he was being taken out, he was serenaded by the fans with a rendition of "The Old Gray Mare." Paige went on to pitch one more year of minor-league ball. It was Paige who said, "How old would you be if you didn't know how old you was?"

- ➢ Other baseball professionals played into their later years: Julio Franco (49), Hoyt Wilhelm (49), Jamie Moyer (49), Phil Niekro (48), Nolan Ryan, Jesse Orosco, Charlie Hough, Tommy John, Randy Johnson (all 46).
- ➢ Gordie Howe, four-time Stanley Cup winner, six-time Hart Trophy (league MVP), six-time Art Ross Trophy (league leading scorer), retired at age 52.
- ➢ Kevin Willis, NBA champion and All-Star, scoring over 17,500 points and grabbing nearly 12,000 rebounds in his career, retired at age 44.
- ➢ In deference to having grown up in St. Louis during the Stan Musial era, I need to include him here. "The Man" retired just before his 43rd birthday in 1963, after a 22-year Hall of Fame career, all with the Cardinals, only three of which he was not an All-Star, and in which he still hit .294 over his final three years.

I retired at age 55, yet I have high school classmates who were still working when we recently celebrated out 70th birthday together. Each of them I have talked to about it tell me that they know retirement is coming. In fact, on the afternoon of writing this section of the book, I am having coffee with a classmate who asked to get together, saying, "I'm probably going to retire in the next year or two, and I'm really concerned. I've been so wrapped up in my work, I haven't thought about what I'm going to do with my time. Can you help?"

Whether at the ripe old athletic age of 43, like NBA Hall-of-Famer, Robert Parish, or the more typical age of 31 for NFL Hall-of-Famer, Barry Sanders, or whether in the older generation retiring at 55 or working into their 70's or 80's, the eventual retirement will come for any number of reasons, associated with injury/health, personal choice, or deselection.

Injury/Health

Some athletic injuries take a while to have their ultimate effect; others have an immediate impact.

➢ Boston Bruin's Marc Savard was averaging nearly 90 points per season, when in March 2010 he sustained a severe concussion in a game against the Penguins. He returned later that season, but he suffered another concussion in January 2011 at age 33, and has not played since.

➢ Bo Jackson, arguably one of the greatest athletes of all time, had promising beginnings of both professional baseball and football careers. During a 1990 NFL playoff game, Jackson, playing for the Oakland Raiders, was tackled from behind, dislocating his hip and ending his football career at age 28. He continued to play baseball, but he could never return to pre-injury form and retired at age 31.

➢ Red Sox star Tony Conigliaro was hit by a pitch just below his eye socket in 1967, during which he made the All-Star team. He returned to the game nearly two years later, but continuing deterioration of his vision forced his retirement after the 1971 season, at age 26. A 1975 comeback attempt ended after 21 games.

➢ Dario Franchitti, four-time IndyCar champion and tied for eighth all-time with 31 career wins and 33 pole positions, went airborne in his car at the 2013 Houston Grand Prix. At age 40, Franchitti, who was expecting to be back the following year, suffered a broken back and right ankle and a concussion. He retired, announcing he was no longer able to compete.

➢ Olympic medalist, Australian swimmer, Emon Sullivan, retired in 2014 at the age of 28, due to a chronic shoulder injury. "In the end my body has let me down, so I'm very disappointed, but it's the right time."

You get the idea—regardless of the sport, the age, and the relative success of the athlete, injuries can and do end careers.

Health issues have a similar effect on the older generations. The National Institute of Aging/National Institutes of Health conducts an extensive ongoing Health and Retirement Study. It has found that for those who have retired between the ages of 55 and 59, 35% reported that poor health was very important to their decision.

Personal Choice

Many athletes leave their sport on their own terms, still young and healthy enough to play, and still able to compete at a high level.

➢ Bobby Jones was one of the great golfers of all time. In 1930, he was 28 and at the peak of his game, winning all of that year's Grand Slam events. When the season was over, he explained that he was choosing to retire to escape the pressure of the game, "Why should I punish myself like this over a golf tournament? Sometimes I'd pass my mother and dad on the course, look at them and not ever see them, because I was so concentrated on the game."

➢ Rocky Marciano had amassed a career record of 49-0 with 43 of the victories coming by knockout. His last fight, at age 31, was in September 1955 at Yankee Stadium, where he knocked out Archie Moore in the ninth. Still fit and fully able to compete, Marciano announced his retirement in April 1956, "...the ring has seen the last of me...and I am not afraid of the future."

➢ Lorena Ochoa had been the number one female golfer in the world, was four-time LPGA Tour Player of the Year, and was earning more than $4 million a season, when she retired in 2010 at age 28. "...it was really clear to see that I didn't want to be out there, you know. I just was thinking of other things. I wanted to get home. I wanted to start working on the foundation. I wanted to be here close to my family."

➢ When he retired from the NFL in 1965 at age 29, Jim Brown had been three-time league MVP and held the career record for rushing yards. In his note to Cleveland owner Art Modell, Brown wrote, "This decision is final and is made only because of the future I desire for myself, my family, and if not to sound corny, my race."

When to retire is not an easy decision for any athlete or older non-athlete to make. In Chapter 8, we will take a look at an approach that both generations can use to decide the right time to retire on their own terms.

Deselection

In their "Athletic Career Programme" that includes a section called "Managing De-Selection" the International Olympic Committee defines "de-selection" as "...when athletes are excluded from a team or a sporting programme based on a decision of exterior parties (or factors), for instance the team's coach, the sports federation, etc." They go on to say, "Generally, athletes are de-selected for reasons that are out of their direct control, such as...age,...inferior performance level compared to other athletes, change of coach..."

As noted earlier, we do not typically use the word "deselection" in hot-stove league conversation. Rather, we use phrases and words like, "being cut," "not being picked up on waivers," "released," and "traded."

Deselection can happen at any level. High school players may not make a college team. For example, of the nearly 475,000 high school baseball players that play each year, less than 7% will play college ball, and just over 3% of the nearly 550,000 high school basketball players each year will play at the next level.

Only a very small percentage of college student-athletes go on to professional or Olympic careers. The funnel gets very narrow. For example, there are over 1.1 million high school football players each year, and fewer than 68,000 will play at the college level. Of those playing in college, just over 250 will be drafted into the pros each year. You do the math—the percentages are incredibly small.

Said another way, among the five major men's team sports in the U. S., football, baseball, hockey, basketball, and soccer, there are fewer than 5,000 total team roster positions available in any year with fewer than 1,100 draft slots. Deselection abounds.

When deselection happens to the elite professional athlete, it can, and perhaps should, lead to retirement, but it doesn't always work that way immediately.

> Steve Carlton began his Hall-of-Fame major league pitching career (four-time Cy Young Award winner, two-time World Series champion, five-time strikeout leader) at age 20, and through age 39, had a win-loss record with the Cardinals and the Phillies of 313-207.

He then went 1-8 with the Phillies at age 40, and finished his career with four other teams from 1986 to 1988, during which he was 15-29. In 1989, the closest Carlton got to interest from a major league team was the Yankees offering him use of their spring training facilities but without an offer to join the spring training team.

➢ Landon Donovan was informed by head coach Jurgen Klinsmann that he would not be on the roster for the June 2014 United States World Cup soccer team. Despite believing he was fit to play and that Klinsmann's decision was a mistake, Donovan, whose professional and international soccer career was exemplary by any standard, had to abide by the coach's choice.

➢ Johnny Unitas had a classic Hall-of-Fame NFL career, passing for more than 40,000 yards, winning a Super Bowl, being selected NFL MVP four times, and being chosen as a Pro Bowl quarterback ten times. After sitting out most of 1968 rehabbing an injury, Unitas had a couple of reasonable, but inconsistent years before spending two more years sharing QB time with the Colts. At age 40, he was traded to the San Diego Chargers, his first year outside the Baltimore organization. After a 1-3 record with the Chargers, he was replaced as the starting quarterback and retired after the year.

➢ AL batting champion, five-time All-Star, four-time World Series champion, and four-time Gold Glove Award winner, centerfielder Bernie Williams played his entire career with the New York Yankees. After 2006, his 16th season, the Yankees offered the 38-year old an opportunity to come to spring training with no guarantee. Williams, who wanted a guaranteed contract and being unwilling to accept a minor league deal, declined the offer. He said, "You want to get out of the game ideally on your own terms. To me, that's the most important thing. If you are forced out of the game, I think you go through a deeper process of having regrets. Eventually, you get over it, but in an ideal world, you want to set up a time and a place in which you can go out on your own terms and then feel fine with it."

Deselection happens for non-athletes as well. We call it downsizing, cutbacks, layoffs, or firings. Just as is true when careers are cut short by injury or poor health, deselection is sudden and certainly not on one's own terms.

Hooker/Solicitor

What is the significance of recognizing that retirement is inescapable? It is not only to acknowledge the fact, but also as a call to action to anticipate and act on the inevitability while still competing.

Isn't anticipation one of the key strengths of a successful athlete or non-athlete? Don't you anticipate the opponent's next football play, baseball pitch, race tactic, boxing move, or tennis serve? Don't you anticipate the competition's next sales promotion or new product technology? Don't you anticipate how a patient will respond to treatment, how a class will do on a test, or how a customer or client will respond to a proposal?

Using those same anticipation skills to recognize that retirement is inevitable and to make plans for it well in advance will increase your odds of success.

Brian Moore is both a hooker and a solicitor. Okay, for all of you non-British sports fans, he has nothing to do with prostitution. Moore was one of Britain's most successful rugby players, and his position was called "hooker." Look it up. And a "solicitor" is an "attorney." Moore, who retired from his sport in 1995 at age 33, is also an author and sports commentator.

He has interviewed many British elite athletes and has been interested in their transitions into retirement. Moore has concluded, "What...clearly emerges from anecdotal and empirical evidence is that those who cope best with the problem of sporting retirement are those who at least give some thought and planning to it before they bow out."

Jerry Reuss
Major League Pitcher
"If I weren't here now, what would I be doing?"

In 1980, Dodger lefthander Jerry Reuss had a career year, 18-6 with a 2.51 ERA, six shutouts, and a no-hitter against the Giants. He views that no-hitter as being better than a perfect game, as the only base runner came as the result of an error, and Reuss says, "I got 28 outs that day; a perfect game is only 27." Reuss finished second to Steve Carlton in the National League Cy Young voting and got the win in the All-Star game, striking out each of the three batters he faced.

A year later, his ERA was down to 2.30, and he had an exemplary post-season. Reuss pitched in two of the five National League Division Series games against the Astros, allowing no runs over 18 innings. In game two, he pitched nine shutout innings before his Dodgers lost 1-0 in the 11th. Then he clinched the best-of-five series by beating Nolan Ryan and the Astros with a complete game shutout. He went on to be game-5 World Series winner as the Dodgers beat the Yankees in six games. Reuss reports that winning the World Series in '81 was "without a doubt" the greatest thrill of his career.

But that career is defined as much by its longevity as by Reuss's spectacular 1980 and 1981 seasons. Through the twentieth century, the mean career length for a major league baseball position player was 5.6 years and for pitchers, it was 4.8 years. Reuss, by contrast, is one of only 29 players in major league history who played in four decades—his rookie year with the Cardinals in 1969 and his retirement year with the Pirates in 1990. He is one of only two pitchers in history (and the winningest, having 220 career victories to Milt Pappas's 209) to collect more than 200 wins without winning 20 or more in any one season. As of this writing, Reuss is number 77 on the all-time wins list, ahead of such notables as Curt Schilling, Jim Perry, Don Drysdale, Bob Lemon, Orel Hershiser, Sandy Koufax, and Lew Burdette.

At age 37, Reuss was plagued by elbow soreness and eventually had surgery. Through 1986 and 1987, struggling to regain his velocity and learning to change speeds, he was 6-16 with an ERA near 6.00. After a great comeback year in 1988 (13-9 with an ERA under 3.50), Reuss went 9-9 with an ERA about 5.00 over what would be the final two years of his career.

To his credit, he did not let retirement sneak up and surprise him. In his mid-30s, on days he was not pitching, Reuss would be in the dugout asking himself, "If I weren't here now, what would I be doing?"

Knowing that his first passion was baseball and wanting to stay in the game, he began to make inquiries about the possibility of joining the media as a way to stay in the sport. When he retired at age 41, Reuss joined ESPN as a broadcaster and has been announcing major and minor league games ever since. He still does radio and TV analysis and play-by-play for the AAA Las Vegas 51's.

Broadcasting is not the only way Reuss has stayed connected to his baseball passion in retirement. He has been a minor league pitching coach for the Expos, Cubs, and Mets. He collects baseball books and CDs. And he authored his baseball autobiography, *Bring in the Right Hander! My Twenty-Two Years in the Major Leagues.*

Ruess also knows that fulfillment in retirement comes from pursuing more than a single passion. It comes from having a holistic set of satisfying activities, and that is what he has created. He is an avid photographer and stays current with emerging technologies, especially those that support his photography hobby. Reuss is also an enthusiastic music collector and listener with a penchant for a wide variety of songs from the '60s. And he thoroughly enjoys his family, which includes seven grandchildren.

What should you be doing during the "Inevitability" phase?
➢ Develop your retirement game plan (Chapters 4 and 5)
➢ Build your retirement team (Chapter 6)
➢ Practice retirement (Chapter 7)
➢ Decide when to retire (Chapter 8)

Retirement Phase 2
Transition

It was inevitable. Yesterday, you were steeped in your profession. Today, you are retired. As an athlete, you might relish a break from the workout grind, the soreness of relentless practices, the long travel stints, aggressive reporters and what they have been writing about you, and that demanding coach. As a non-athlete, you might enjoy a break from the business grind, the stress of providing services to those in great and constant need, work travel, rush hour traffic, and that demanding boss. You might even experience a period, albeit likely a very brief one, of euphoria.

Despite a feeling of relief from some of the demands of your career, it would be normal for the predominant sense to be that there a hole in your life. You have lost what was familiar; the things that just showed up every day while you were still competing that are no longer there the day after you retire.

Caroline Silby, sports psychologist in Bethesda, Maryland, shares her experience dealing with retired competitors, "A lot of athletes will tell you they're relieved, but when you start pulling back the layers, they start to also experience this sense of loss."

At the beginning of this phase, it's important to recognize that managing through transition is about you and those closest to you. It is not about your former team, league, sport, job, or company. The cruel reality is that despite how much you were valued and loved in your former role, it will all go on without you.

On my last day of work, my replacement, Dan Price, and I were sitting in "his" office after a long day of meetings. It was about 6:30pm, and we had been at it since 7:00 that morning. Dan sounded blunt, but I value to this day what he said. It changed my mindset and enabled me to begin to focus on "my" retirement, "Al, why don't you go home. Tomorrow we need to do this without you, and we will."

Thank you, Dan.

There are a number of classic ways that people have characterized the timeframe during which we leave the familiar behind and move on:

> Elisabeth Kubler-Ross characterizes the stages of dealing with death and dying: denial, anger, bargaining, and depression, before reaching "acceptance"
> John James and Russell Friedman describe the grief recovery process, the complex emotions we experience when dealing with loss before reaching "completeness"
> William Bridges helps individuals and organizations manage transition associated with change by recognizing the end of the old and living in a neutral zone before reaching the "new beginning"

> ➤ In *Your Retirement Quest,* Keith Lawrence and I describe the stages after your retirement day as moving from a honeymoon period through disenchantment to rejuvenation before reaching "fulfillment"

Each of these approaches is based on the same principles. When we leave that familiar part of our lives behind, it is natural to experience a time of complex emotions and their effects, some of which can be risky. If we acknowledge the reality of the loss; recognize and accept the normality of the emotions and address them; actively look for and discover the new possibilities; and be intentional about planning for our future; we increase the odds of creating the new life we desire and deserve. Whether we call it acceptance, completeness, new beginning, or fulfillment, it is what we are striving for.

William Bridges' word "transition" works best for me to characterize this phase of retirement in that it captures the dynamism of the journey. One definition reads, "the process or a period of changing from one state or condition to another."

Jenny Owens, Australian Olympic skier, recognized the value of the dynamic transition and wrote, "The transition to 'real life' is...difficult because of the sudden cut-off of the intense demands of elite athletic performance. When you combine that with the sudden loss of the intense devotion to professional competition and its rewards, it's a significant shift in all sorts of ways."

By contrast, a *Harvard Business Review* article shared a case study that describes someone who did not approach retirement as a dynamic transition to a positive future, but rather became stagnant, "A retired CEO, Jerry was a sad, aging man who reflected constantly on the emptiness of his life...For people like Jerry the public recognition that accompanies a position at the top...becomes the most meaningful dimension of their lives...With retirement, all these anchors disappear from one day to the next."

The power is in facing the reality of change and leaning into the future, recognizing the transition will be dynamic.

Kim Ensing
Collegiate Basketball Player
"more painful not to play"

Kim Ensing is the Athletic Director at Allan Hancock College in Santa Maria, California. She works with college athletes every day, and they are fortunate to benefit from her perspective. Ensing's own college basketball career was cut short by a serious back injury incurred during a practice scrimmage. The pain in her back was severe, but Ensing says, "I still tried to re-enter play even against doctor's orders. It was more painful not to play."

In recalling that time in her life, she uses words like depressing, agonizing, hopelessness, and devastating to describe the realization that she would not return to the court.

Although to this day, Ensing deals with some neurological incapacity, she has had the personal strength to turn challenge into opportunity. Wanting to stay connected to her sport, she set her sights on coaching. And wanting to learn more about the effects on athletes when they leave their sport, she conducted a study that became the basis for her Master's thesis in Athletic Administration. She conducted and analyzed extensive interviews with 12 female athletes whose college sports careers had ended.

Ensing summarizes her findings concisely, indicating that each interviewee experienced grief in response to the loss of her athletic career, and she believes it was cathartic for her to recognize that she was not alone in grieving for the loss of her sport. The research helped her move on, and refocusing on coaching led to her current Athletic Director role, where she has the opportunity to help today's student-athletes plan for their transitions. Despite her desire to help in that regard, she admits that resources and information are still sadly lacking.

Your opportunity during the transition phase is to acknowledge and address the losses and natural emotions you are experiencing. Despite the discomfort, this is a time to redefine yourself. Hopefully, you had already begun to develop your game plan, to build your team, and to practice during the inevitability phase. But even if you hadn't, you can and should do so now.

The risk of the transition phase is that you don't address the losses and emotions, and you languish there for much too long. The result of doing so can be devastating. This is when some of the major issues, such as those experienced by McMahon, Walker, Jarrett, Irabu, and Hatton, can take over lives.

Two more points about transition—first, it can begin even before you retire. Had Carlton, Donovan, Unitas, and Williams already begun their transition while they were still playing? As the inevitability sinks in, the emotions of the transition phase can begin early.

Secondly, the emotions of transition can return even after you have thought you have left them behind.

Dan Batsch
College Football Player
"In hindsight..."

Dan Batsch played pee-wee football in his hometown of Cape Girardeau, Missouri and his prep ball at Lakota High School in a Cincinnati, Ohio suburb. By high school, he had recognized that he had the skills and size to be more than just another player, and he dedicated himself on the practice field, in the weight room, and on game day to do what it took to be successful.

After a great high school career, Dan went on to red-shirt his freshmen year and then start for four years as an outside linebacker, defensive end, and defensive tackle at the University of Wisconsin.

His college career was sufficiently successful, as measured by tackles, fumbles caused and recovered (for which he still holds the Wisconsin career record), and sacks, that he was optimistic about the possibility of being drafted. Before leaving on winter break his senior year, Dan's position coach told him that he felt he had a shot. When Dan returned from the break, however, that message had changed.

In retrospect, Dan believes there were two reasons he was not drafted. One was his combination of size and speed. Although he was large by normal standards, he had difficulty maintaining weight each season, typically starting at 270 but falling off to 245-ish. And although fast enough to compete in college, he believes NFL teams thought his speed would not be adequate at the next level. In addition, he had experienced a long string of injuries through his career, knee, shoulder, hamstring, and hip. The NFL may not have been willing to invest in someone with a risky health pedigree.

Despite not being drafted, Dan struggled to hold on to his dream of playing professionally and fully considered pursuing it through free agency, but in the end, chose not to do so. He knew in his heart of hearts that there was a better-than-average chance he would not have made it. And he was in a no-lose situation.

While at Wisconsin, Dan had not only been focused on football—he had earned his mechanical engineering degree. Dan credits his ability to do both at a high level to having learned discipline, dedication, time management, and priority setting; all life skills that still serve him well. He has parlayed the degree into a great corporate career while also building a wonderful family with his wife, Julie.

Dan's ability to create a full and fulfilling life after football can be attributed to assuring that he had a strong non-football life plan for when the time inevitably came to hang up his cleats. Dan played his last game in 1990 but still says, "In hindsight, I do wish I had given it a chance and tried free agency."

Those normal and natural feelings of loss may return, even in the best of circumstances.

What should you be doing during the "Transition" phase?

If you've not done so already:

➢ Develop your retirement game plan (Chapters 4 and 5)
➢ Build your retirement team (Chapter 6)

But also:

➢ Make game plan adjustments (Chapter 9)

Retirement Phase 3
Engagement

In their book, *The Grief Recovery Handbook*, authors John James and Russell Friedman make it clear it is unfortunate that we are taught at a young age that one way to recover from grief is to "replace the loss." They tell James's story—when he was a boy, his beloved dog died. He grieved. He cried. His father said, "Don't cry—on Saturday, we'll get you a new dog."

Certainly, in the case of the loss of a loved one, a spouse, a parent, a child, or even a family pet, it is impossible to really "replace the loss." Recovery from that kind of loss, that source of grief, cannot be achieved by remarrying or having another child or buying a new dog. It requires a deeper emotional process, and their book provides just such an approach.

But with all due respect to James and Friedman, I contend that for the kinds of losses associated with the retirement of an elite athlete or a career-dedicated older non-athlete, replacing the losses is, in fact, the work of retirement game planning. And I contend that as you begin to replace what you have lost, it is then that you can and will fully engage in your new phase of life.

"Love life. Engage in it. Give it all you've got. Love it with a passion because life truly does give back, many times over, what you put into it." This is but one of countless inspirational thoughts from the late Maya Angelou, celebrated poet and civil rights activist, among her many achievements.

Ms. Angelou's few sentences eloquently restate the vision for our lives that we established earlier, a vision that bears repeating in the context of her words.

Envision a time in your life when you are full of energy and contented at the same time. Your life is full of close relationships with family and friends; you are contributing your time and resources to helping others; your days, weeks, months, and years are filled with activities that you love, that help you grow, and that are just plain fun. You awaken each day with a positive attitude about life and are clear about your life's purpose and your personal values. You have the resources and general well-being to live the life that makes you happy and can foresee living it well into your future.

You take advantage of new-found opportunities, and you deal with life's inevitable setbacks, because you are resilient and have a plan that helps guide you through them.

Envision a time when you are fully engaged in life. Thank you, Ms. Angelou.

Engagement is the third phase of retirement, and the good news is that you can accelerate getting there by taking the right steps in the first two phases, inevitability and transition. We will delve into how to do that, but for now, we'll look a little more deeply into the engagement phase.

The Health and Retirement Study we referred to earlier surveys a representative sample of approximately 20,000 people over the age of 50 every two years. Not surprisingly, the study has found that "engaged retirees are significantly more likely to be satisfied with retirement than their non-engaged counterparts, regardless of age, sex, race, marital status, education, mental or physical health, or income."

Although this study is conducted for older Americans, it seems intuitive that the concept applies to younger retirees as well. We already learned about Koufax, Prince, Sorenstam, Lawrence, Brown, Bly, Spitz, and Arnold; all fully engaged in life in retirement.

Add to that list the retired athletes whose profiles you will find throughout the book:

> ➤ Cindy Rarick—Professional Golf: vintner
> ➤ Dan Batsch—College Football: corporate engineer, raising a family
> ➤ Dan Cross—Professional Basketball: runs summer basketball camps, manages a foundation helping athletes transition to new careers
> ➤ Don Davey—Professional Football: founded and manages financial advising firm, raising a family, owns fast food franchises, runs foundation helping athletes transition out of their sports, manages a real estate investment firm, volunteers for multiple charities, triathlete
> ➤ Garrett Broshuis—Professional Baseball: attorney, writer for *Baseball America*, raising a family

> ➤ Jerry Ruess—Professional Baseball: author, baseball book collector, music aficionado, photographer, grandfather
> ➤ Julie Isphording—Olympic Marathoner: public speaker, syndicated radio host, 10K race director, author, leadership and training consultant
> ➤ Ken Holtzman—Professional Baseball: stock broker, health and physical education director, grandfather
> ➤ Kim Ensing—College Basketball: athletic director
> ➤ Pete Woods—Professional Football: attorney, community activist, Vice President local chapter NFL Retired Players Association

To be clear, engaging in your new life doesn't mean completely forgetting the old one. In fact, there is some value in holding on to pieces of the old, but respecting and building on your past doesn't mean dwelling on or wallowing in it.

I have memories from my career with Procter & Gamble around the house. My 33 years working there made up a meaningful part of my life that I cherish. I've kept a copy of the patent on which I am a co-inventor, some of the awards I won, photos with esteemed work colleagues, and other items. When I pass by them, it feels good, but I don't sit staring in self-pity thinking about the good old days. No time for that.

Displaying your trophies and memorabilia? Sure. Keeping retirement gifts? Yes. Honoring the past? Absolutely. Wallowing? Not allowed!

What should you be doing during the "Engagement" phase?

If you have not done so already:

> ➤ Develop your retirement game plan (Chapters 4 and 5)
> ➤ Build your retirement team (Chapter 6)

If you have your plan, live it and love it.

And make game plan adjustments (Chapter 9)

Retirement Phase 4
Second Retirement
(For the Elite Athlete Only)

Inevitability→Transition→Engagement, the three phases of retirement, sometimes and, perhaps, preferably overlapping. These apply to elite athletes and non-athletes of the older generation. For elite athletes, however, there is a fourth phase.

Although each of you will experience your unique life path, consider this possible and perhaps probable scenario. You have dedicated yourself to your sport since the age of seven, and you retired from your sport in your early 20s at the end of your collegiate career or a bit older, having retired from a professional or Olympic career.

You moved through the transition phase and engaged in a new life and a second career, knowing that you still had decades to live the meaningful life you aspired to. You may have been working in real estate, insurance, education. You may have stayed in your sport in some capacity like coaching or broadcasting. You may have dedicated your time, talent, and treasure to giving back to others through a foundation or in support of a cause that is important to you. There are as many options for you as there would have been were you to have entered this career without having ever been an elite athlete.

You applied yourself to this second career as you applied yourself to your athletic career. And you have now done so for 30 or 40 or more years. Now you are at a life stage where those older non-athlete retirees we have been referring to are today.

You will go through the first three phases of retirement again. This "second retirement" is your fourth phase. But you have an advantage. You will have practiced retirement once. Your opportunity is to have learned from your first experience—to start early to create the game plan for this next retirement. You know that doing so will minimize the time to get fully engaged after retirement number two.

Brett Hull retired from his 19-year NHL career in 2005, having scored nearly 1,400 points, more than his number of games played, including 741 goals, which is third all-time. He was inducted into the Hall of Fame in

2009. Hull is now an executive vice-president in the St. Louis Blues front office. Hull will inevitably retire from that career as well. When he does, he'll be transitioning through phase 4.

Hall-of-Fame pitcher Jim Bunning has retired from politics, his second career. Six-time Pro-Bowl offensive lineman Dan Dierdorf has retired from broadcasting, his second career. Olympic skating medal winner, Tenley Albright retired from her work as a surgeon, her second career.

Your second retirement is inevitable; you will go through a transition; and then if you have done the game planning, built your new retirement team, and practiced, you will be fully engaged, living the older retirement you deserve.

Where do we go from here?

We have spent the first three chapters understanding the retirement playing field. You have had a chance to think about the losses that may be in front of you or which you are dealing with now. You understand that retirement is inevitable and that the best time to begin putting your game plan together is now, regardless of where you are in your life journey.

You know that you will experience losses and deal with the complex emotions as you transition from the familiarity of your primary career to your new future. And you should be encouraged by the opportunity to engage with life in new ways and live a fulfilling vision you can create for yourself and strive for.

It is time to begin putting your game plan in place.

The Game Plan

You have a good feel for the retirement playing field, and it is time to take the next steps to establish your retirement game plan. When you are an elite athlete competing on the field, court, pitch, track, ice, or course, you need to understand what it will take to win and sustain your success over the long haul—world-class technique, strong offense, rock solid defense, a talented bench, good coaching, and so on. These are the key elements you need to put in place.

When you are competing in the products or services marketplace, you need to understand what it will take to yield great results and sustain your success over the long haul—world-class quality, timely and caring customer service, a talented and motivated organization, good leadership, and so on. These are the key elements you need to put in place.

Knowing the key elements is necessary but not sufficient. Great players and teams and great companies, executives, teachers, lawyers, doctors, and other professionals also candidly assess themselves on each of these important factors. They know where they are strong, so they can build a game plan to take advantage, and they know where they are weak, so they can work diligently to improve.

As I'm sure you have guessed by now, there are also key elements that will yield a successful retirement and sustain it over the long haul. In this section of the book, we will identify and describe each of these key elements, give you the opportunity to candidly assess whether each is a strength or weakness for you, and give you several approaches to use your assessment to devise your personal retirement game plan.

Having that game plan is necessary but not sufficient. A game plan is only as good as the team effort that goes into creating and executing it. Even athletes who compete as individuals, like tennis players, golfers, sprinters, and boxers, have teams that support them. Even non-athlete professionals that work individually with clients, customers, students, or patients, have teams that support them. To be successful, everyone on the team needs to play their role and be on the same game plan.

Who's on your retirement team and are they all on the same page?

Chapter 4

Strengths and Weaknesses

"Success is where preparation and opportunity meet."
Bobby Unser (and others)

"...you are an athlete. When this comes to an end,
how do you adapt to the change?"
Emily Brunemann

When I was working with my coauthor Keith Lawrence to write *Your Retirement Quest*, we used the retirement-relevant research and hundreds of interviews to identify the ten key elements of a fulfilling retirement. Since we developed the list about a decade ago, it has stood the test of time for a wide range of people interested in creating a more successful new future.

We have presented the key element concepts to nearly 10,000 Boomers, to groups in their 40s, to older seniors, to employees of companies, to retired clergy, to clients of financial firms, and we were even asked to present to Boy Scouts, because said the person who asked, "These key elements are about life in general, not just retirement."

We have had several workshops in which a grandchild, a 20-something, brought a grandparent and sat through the session. In each case, the young person came up to us afterward and expressed how much they got out of it, because the key elements applied to them.

In the context of this book, I'm confident you'll find the key elements apply to you as well, whether you are a young elite athlete or an older non-athlete.

For the remainder of this chapter, I'll review each key element, what it is and why it's important. At the end of each key element description, you will find a statement about the element. Think about how it applies to you and whether it is a strength or weakness. This is your opportunity to candidly assess yourself relative to that key element and in doing so, build the foundation of your retirement game plan. For your assessment, use a scale of 1 to 5.

> 1=I have given this key element very little, if any, thought.
>
> 2=I have thought about this key element before, but it's a real improvement opportunity for me.
>
> 3=There are some things about this key element that are working for me, but it could use some improvement.
>
> 4=I have a lot going for me in this key element, and I can improve even further with a little attention.
>
> 5=I have this key element in full control and am very satisfied with it.

I want to emphasize the word, "candidly." In the same way that you would not want to kid yourself about a strength or weakness in your sports or business game planning, you do not want to do so here. Although you might eventually want to share your assessment with your retirement teammates, for now, your assessment is for your personal use. Be honest with yourself, and your retirement game plan will be the better for it.

One final point before we go on. I have numbered the key elements for reference only. They are not presented in any order of importance, nor is the list a menu from which to choose. Although you will likely set some priorities on the order in which you work on them, eventually bringing all of the key elements into your game plan, into your life, is the magic. We will revisit this point later as you build your game plan.

Key Element #1
Life Purpose

"Efforts and courage are not enough without purpose and direction."
John F. Kennedy

"A life is not important except in the impact it has on other lives."
Jackie Robinson

And one more...

*"The two most important days in your life
are the day you are born and the day you find out why."*
Mark Twain

At any given time, we play one or more roles in our lives—mother, QB, teacher, point guard, VP, miler, brother, doctor, hooker, solicitor, coach... Then, inevitably, that role changes or in the case of retirement, disappears.

You may have never heard of Buckminster Fuller—he was a futurist, author, architect, and inventor, who died in 1983. When he was a young man, his six-year old daughter died of complications from polio and spinal meningitis. During that dark period, he began a philosophical search for his life purpose and concluded that it was to add value to and improve the quality of people's lives on earth. He made it his life's work to discover how much one person could contribute to changing the world and benefitting humanity.

When describing his philosophy to others, he used the simple analogy of the honeybee. The work of the bee, its role, is to collect nectar from flowers to take back to the hive for the production of honey. Fuller observed that the bee's higher purpose is more than nectar collection and honey making. It is to help sustain life on earth by cross-pollinating the flowers.

I believe Fuller would argue that if bees could think, they would be satisfied to know that their role, the work they do, is aligned with their life purpose. That is the power of taking the time to understand, articulate, and live your life purpose. When you choose activities that are consistent with your reason for being, doing so will serve both to fulfill that purpose and to increase your personal satisfaction.

If you have not identified your life purpose, there are things you can do to get started:

➤ Envision a time when your 15-year-old grandchild asks you, "Grandma (or Grandpa), what has your life been all about?" It is not likely that you will tell him or her exclusively that you were an

Olympic gymnast, a corporate executive, or a collegiate hockey player. What will you answer them in language they could understand?

➤ If you had complete freedom and were told you had a year to live, what would you do with your remaining time and, more importantly, why?

➤ There are a number of on-line sites that can help get you started—one example is the Franklin Covey Mission Statement Builder.

Some examples of life purpose statements I've come across:

➤ "Enable dreams"
➤ "Energize and inspire purpose in others"
➤ "Be a catalyst for positive change"
➤ "Live and mentor an authentic, spiritual life"
➤ "Reconciliation"

My statement is "Living my parents' legacy." I strive to do this both for myself and for passing it along to others.

The key is to identify the life purpose that is meaningful for you and to align your activities to be consistent with that purpose.

LIFE PURPOSE ASSESSMENT: Candidly assess yourself on the 1-to-5 scale for the following statement:

If not yet retired

I am clear on life purpose—I have a list of activities planned for retirement that are consistent with that purpose.

If already retired

I am clear on life purpose—I have aligned my life's activities to be consistent with that purpose.

Assessment Rating: _____

Key Element #2
Passions

---

*"Passion is one great force that unleashes creativity,
because if you're passionate about something, then you're more willing to take risks."*

Yo-Yo Ma

"If you don't love what you do, you won't do it with much conviction or passion."

Mia Hamm

You have been passionate about your career. What happens when that career is behind you? Al Iafrate retired from a 13-year NHL career as a defenseman at age 32, and he made it clear, "It's hard to replace the passion you have for a sport."

He may be right that "it's hard," but finding those new passions is well worth the effort. Have you taken the time to think about the following questions?

- ➤ What will I do in retirement that will be so exciting for me that it will cause me to lose track of time?
- ➤ What will I be doing that I will be excited to tell others about?
- ➤ What will be on my list of activities that will make me want to jump out of bed to get started in the morning?
- ➤ What will I be doing that piques my curiosity and causes me to constantly want to learn more, do more, and get better?

This key element has two components, understanding what you are passionate about, those things you love to do, and then actually pursuing them.

Cindy Rarick retired from a successful 23-year LPGA career at age 48. Her new passion is the winery she began with her partner, Gary Seidler. Silvara Vineyards is in the state of Washington, where Cindy spends her summers, while spending her winters in Arizona.

I retired at age 55 from a 33-year career as a corporate executive. I am doing one of my passions right now—this is my sixth book. I write virtually every day, and I've been doing that since beginning to work on my first book in 2005. This morning, I was pursuing another of my passions, baseball. I play in a 60-year old and over league in the summer, although I need a 70-and-over league to play with "kids my own age," and we began winter indoor practice.

Dikembe Mutombo was 42 when he retired from his 18-season NBA career. Since then, he has focused his energies on his humanitarian work, including the completion and opening of the Biamba Marie Mutombo Hospital. The hospital, named for his mother who died of a stroke, is on the outskirts of Kinshasa, the Congolese capital and Mutombo's hometown. He is passionate about his community and about his mother.

One other question you might ask yourself is, "What did I love to do when I was ten years old?" When we're ten, we're old enough to make choices about what we enjoy doing. As we get older, perhaps other things in life get in the way of pursuing our passions. Retirement can be an opportunity to return to those ten-year-old's passions. These will not likely be the only things on your passions-potentials list, but you might be surprised how well they fit into your retirement life.

> PASSIONS ASSESSMENT: Candidly assess yourself on the 1-to-5 scale for the following statement:

> <u>If not yet retired</u>
> **I know what will keep me excited about my life in retirement and what activities I will enthusiastically pursue.**

If already retired

I am excited about my life and the many activities I enthusiastically pursue.

Assessment Rating: _____

Key Element #3
Attitude

"Attitude is a little thing that makes a big difference."
Winston Churchill

"It's not whether you get knocked down; it's whether you get up."
Vince Lombardi

Researchers at Wayne State University used photographs from a 1952 player registry to study the longevity of major league baseball players it related to their happiness. The sole measure of each player's fundamental level of happiness, what the researchers referred to as "general underlying disposition," was the intensity and sincerity of their smiles in the photographs. The researchers compared the longevity of the players who had passed away (46 of the 230 were still alive when the study was conducted in June 2009) to their smile intensity level. Players with no smiles on their photos lived an average of 72.9 years; those with partial smiles 75 years; and those with full, sincere smiles lived an average of 79.9 years—a full seven years longer than the no-smile group.

Stop for a moment and think about that. Knowing nothing more than how sincerely happy the players looked in a 1952 photo, the researchers were able to link that level of happiness to a statistically significant difference in longevity, more than four decades later.

Similar studies have been done with comparable longevity results using high school and college senior yearbook photos. The studies have also found correlations to marital satisfaction and divorce rates. Bottom line—attitude, even when measured in the simplest of ways, is a major influencer of longevity and quality of life.

You may want to pull out that year book and take a look.

Attitude can affect your perception of everything from financial security to how you approach relationships; from your ability to have fun to how you approach life in general. You know people who have optimistic, positive, hopeful, engaging attitudes. They are like Tigger from Winnie the Pooh. And you know people who are exactly the opposite. Eeyore.

What are some characteristics of people with positive attitudes? They have and frequently express gratitude. They are warm and welcoming, greeting others with a smile and a "hello." Have you ever met a person for the first time or pass someone you don't know in the hall or on the street and immediately sense that they are the kind of person you want to hang out with?

People with positive attitudes are predisposed to say, "Yes." They anticipate that things will work out well or perhaps, that they will be able to positively influence how things will work out. They are open to opportunities and jump on them with little hesitation. This approach keeps them more engaged in life.

People with positive attitudes are resilient, able to rebound after a setback. During an athlete's playing career, he or she gets innumerable opportunities to exhibit and practice resilience. Sure, elite athletes are winners, but how many games, matches, races, tournaments, or bouts have they lost? Each loss requires resilience to bounce back and get ready for the next competition. Some do this better than others.

Have you noticed that some pitchers who get what they believe is a bad call by a home-plate umpire are able to put it behind them and focus on the next pitch? Others carry the call into the next pitch and even next batter or inning. Which of these is more resilient?

Every non-athlete professional also has setbacks. Those who are most resilient can focus on the solution rather than wallow around in the problem.

A positive attitude, exhibited by resilience, is a key factor in being willing and able to navigate the grief recovery process. For the older retiree, either the non-athlete or eventually the athlete, a positive attitude is invaluable when aging through retirement.

Many believe that attitude is hardwired into our personalities. This is not the case. Here are but a few examples of what you can do to improve your attitude.

➤ Work on gratitude. Begin and end your day by expressing appreciation for all that is right in your life. Say "thank you" more frequently.
  ➤ Surround yourself with a positive environment. Identify and eliminate those things and people that tend to darken your day. Unplug from whatever depletes you.
  ➤ Surround yourself with people who have a positive attitude. It's difficult to have a positive attitude if you are surrounded by Eeyores.
  ➤ Look for or, better yet, create opportunities to do random acts of kindness. These don't have to be big things. Smile at a stranger (by the way, the smile you get back will feel good). Give a sincere compliment. Offer to run an errand for someone who is ill.
  ➤ Watch, read, or listen to someone who is inspiring.

Are you a Tigger or an Eeyore?

ATTITUDE ASSESSMENT: Candidly assess yourself on the 1-to-5 scale for the following statement:

Whether already retired or not
Those closest to me describe me as having a positive attitude. I'm a Tigger.

Assessment Rating: _____

Key Element #4
Financial Security

"Would you rather live like a King for a few years and die broke
or live like a Prince forever?"
The Real Athlete Blog

"Rule No. 1: Never lose money.
Rule No. 2: Never forget Rule No. 1."
Warren Buffett

Based on the 2016-17 scale, the average NBA salary is just over $5,000,000. A lot of money? Yes. Financial security assured? No.

The NBA Players Association and the league itself recognize that the financial situation for the players is very complex, and perhaps more importantly, many young players do not have the knowledge necessary to manage their money. The association and the league have stepped up financial education, including engaging with Personal Capital, to help build knowledge and provide the necessary money management technology.

As part of their work with the NBPA, Personal Capital studied player spending habits and concluded that the average NBA professional spends more than $500,000 per year. Envision a short career, which most of them are. Envision a player not being willing or able to adjust spending during or after his career. The result—financial insecurity.

Now envision an approach to financial security—the primary vehicle being a written financial plan that matches your lifestyle (budget) to your available resources. Note that I did not say that financial security is about how much money you have accumulated. Rather, if you profoundly understand what your resources are and then build a spending plan to live within those resources now and throughout your future, you will be financially secure in the absolute sense, and you will be comfortable that you need not spend all of your time worrying about your finances.

The media is replete with stories of elite athletes who made multi-millions in their careers but have gone bankrupt in relatively short order. Earlier, we referred to the 2009 Sports Illustrated study that found, for example, that a majority of former NFL players had gone bankrupt or were experiencing financial stress within two years of retirement. There are a number of causes for this, but they can be boiled down to each affected individual not having matched his lifestyle to his available resources.

This is not just a problem for athletes. Recall the earlier story of the Baby Boomer couple and their attractive, yet unaffordable, country club lifestyle?

There are two other critical components to achieving real financial security: 1) build the right financial support team, quarterbacked by a trusted advisor who has your best interests at heart, and 2) ensure you and your significant others are aligned to your financial plans.

Let's look at each of these components in a bit more depth. You can choose to manage your own money or seek help from family or friends who may know little more about it than you do. But is that the best path to take? Many financial advisors have financial advisors of their own. I had just assumed that they were the experts—why not just manage their own money? They explain that their advisor provides them with unbiased, unemotional, third-party perspective, which is critical during the ups and downs of investing.

There are two important parts of the advisor equation. First, do your due diligence to ensure you have a financial team you can trust. Second, follow the insight of President Reagan, when he said, "Trust but verify." Stay close to the advisor to make sure you understand and agree with his or her recommendations. We'll revisit this in Chapter 6, in which we'll talk about who should be on your retirement team.

Finally, part of the comfort of knowing you are financially secure derives from being confident that those closest to you, for example, your spouse, partner, or significant other, share your understanding of the financial plan and are comfortable with it. Your financial future may also be contingent on the understanding you have with others you may be supporting, like adult children or aging parents. Have you discussed your financial plans with those closest to you? Are you aligned?

FINANCIAL SECURITY ASSESSMENT: Candidly assess yourself on the 1-to-5 scale for the following statement:

Whether already retired or not

I understand and follow my budget to live within my financial resources. I have a written financial plan, developed with the help of trusted advisors, to enable me to live the life I want, now and into my future. Those closest to me also understand and are comfortable with the financial plan.

Assessment Rating: _____

Garrett Broshuis
Professional Baseball Player
Financial Security—less than minimum wage

Only about 10% of minor league baseball players ever make it to the majors. That being said, those who do not make it have still dedicated their lives to their sport, building skills, making personal sacrifices, and being passionate about pursuing their dream. And their identity is still tied up in the fact that they are professional baseball players. One big difference versus their counterparts who reach the majors is their lack of financial security. Since 1976, major league salaries have increased more than 2,500%, while minor league salaries have increased less than 70%. As of this writing, there are lawsuits in the works that contend that minor leaguers generally make less than minimum wage.

Garrett Broshuis was an All-State basketball and baseball player at Advance High School (Missouri) and his class valedictorian, sporting a 4.0 GPA. The University of Missouri offered him both academic and athletic scholarships, and Garrett jumped at the chance, going on to earn his Bachelor's in Psychology. His pride in having this balance in his life would suit him well as he moved through his baseball career and beyond it.

Garrett's college pitching career included playing with Ian Kinsler and Matt Scherzer, both who went on to be successful major leaguers. His own career at Mizzou was also exemplary. In his senior year, he finished with a perfect 11-0 record, helping lead the Tigers to the NCAA Regionals. This level of performance was no fluke. Like most elite athletes, Garrett combined innate talent with an insatiable drive to succeed. Through his four years of college, he dedicated six to eight hours a day, every day, to honing his skills and fitness.

Garrett also applied his determination to do his best at his studies—he was selected as a first team Academic All-American. His vision was a career doing memory research as well as a career in baseball.

When he was drafted in the fourth round by the San Francisco Giants in 2004, Garrett chose baseball, and it led him to a six-year minor league career during which he progressed to the AAA level. His stats were up and down, leading his league in losses one year and in wins the next. But he continued to put in the effort to achieve his dream of playing in the majors.

During his baseball career, Garrett also knew that regardless of whether or not he made the majors, he would, either by his choice or by someone else's, need to eventually move on to other endeavors. During one off season, Garrett worked in a psychology lab doing the memory research he thought he would want to do in his post-baseball career. He was glad he had practiced retirement, because he discovered this work was not for him. He would need to find something else outside of baseball about which he was passionate.

At the end of spring training for the 2009 season, Garrett was confronted with the opportunity to think more seriously about no longer playing. He was asked to come into the office, where several of the Giants minor league administrators were assembled. He still refers to that meeting as a "punch in my gut" and the beginning of a "very painful day." He was told that he was no longer in the Giants plans for their major league roster, that year or any year. They said he could play out the season, which he chose to do, and he could have even played in subsequent seasons, which he chose, at age 28, not to do.

By that time, Garrett had begun to think about attending law school. During that final season, he spent his free time studying, and the day after the season ended, he took the LSAT's. Three years later, he was his law school valedictorian (sound familiar?) and went on to begin his law career. He was and is moved by something President Gerald Ford said when he lost the election for another term. Ford recognized that it was the end of a long career in politics, and when asked what he would now do with his life, the president said, "I'll find another ladder to climb."

Despite having a clear direction, Garrett still found the transition difficult. He spent six months often reflecting on the word "failure." How would others perceive him now that he was no longer a professional athlete? How would they and he think about his legacy of never having made it to the majors? He credits his wife as being the stabilizing force that got him through his transition into his post-baseball life.

Oh, and about those lawsuits regarding pay for minor leaguers— Attorney Garrett Broshuis is on the front lines of making them happen. He has replaced his passion, still strives to do what it takes to be successful, works to ensure he has balance in his life, and continues to be a fan of the game he loves.

Key Element #5
Giving Back

"Giving back involves a certain amount of giving up."
Colin Powell

"Life's most persistent and urgent question is,
'What are you doing for others?'"
Martin Luther King, Jr.

One does not have to search long to find numerous examples of elite athletes who have created charitable foundations, given their time to help others, and loaned their names to great causes. And we all know of friends and family members from all walks of life who volunteer at food pantries, on non-profit boards, in local hospitals, and many other places where needs are evident.

What is your giving back plan? How will you apply your time, talent, and treasure to make a difference in something larger than yourself? And why should you do it at all?

The "why" question may surprise you. Isn't it evident? Don't our communities need our support? Yes, they do. But there is more to giving back than that.

Warning—we're going to be a bit selfish for a while. There is no doubt that we can do good things for others, but it is also acceptable, in this case, to ask the question, "What's in it for me?" And isn't that what we are thinking about—creating a retirement that is full and fulfilling for each of us?

The research is clear and consistent—those who volunteer get even more satisfaction from their efforts than those they are helping. A corollary of the research findings is that the closer you are to the person you are helping, the greater your personal satisfaction.

Should you support your favorite causes financially? Yes. Should you give your time as well and, perhaps, even more so? Absolutely.

The good news is that giving back is a win-win. The bad news is that a surprisingly small percentage of people who have the time and talent to do so actually step up and volunteer. For example, if you ask Baby Boomers if they plan to volunteer in retirement, about 70% say they will. Less than a third actually do.

Retired major league pitcher, Jamie Moyer and his wife, Karen, established the Moyer Foundation and spend time with the young people at their bereavement camps, where they "provide comfort, hope, and healing to children affected by loss and family addiction."

Former number-two ranked tennis professional, Andrea Jaeger, retired at age 20 due to major shoulder injuries. She dedicated herself to philanthropy and to personally serving others; even before she became a nun. Like the Moyers, Sister Andrea has focused her efforts on helping children in need, creating camping experiences for young cancer patients.

Retired educator, Ronnie Brockman, and her husband, retired sales executive, Allen, are the cofounders and hands-on leaders of Camp Rainbow, which "provides free camping experiences to children undergoing treatment for, and survivors of, cancer and blood-related diseases and disorders."

The Moyers, Sister Jaeger, and the Brockmans are making a difference with their time, talent, and treasure. Although camping for children in need is a common theme across their work, volunteer efforts are needed everywhere. There are innumerable ways to help others and in doing so, help yourself.

> GIVING BACK ASSESSMENT: Candidly assess yourself on the 1-to-5 scale for the following statement:
>
> <u>Whether already retired or not</u>
>
> **I am applying my time, talent, and treasure to make a difference in the lives of others, and in doing so, I am making a positive difference in my life.**
>
> Assessment Rating: _____

Key Element #6
Healthy Relationships

"If I miss anything about sport, it's the camaraderie of old teammates."
Bo Jackson

"We will be friends until forever, just you wait and see."
Winnie the Pooh

We are inundated, and appropriately so, with warnings of the negative effects of smoking, alcoholism, not exercising, and obesity. Yet there is a factor in our lives that has an equivalent effect on our longevity and quality of life that we seldom hear about—the number of and quality of our relationships.

Researchers at Brigham Young University analyzed nearly 150 previously-conducted studies to learn about the effects of "low social interaction" on health and longevity. They conducted the analysis because of the growing concern about significant reductions in the quantity and quality of relationships in industrialized countries. Many things may be contributing—for example, there is a broadly increased reliance on technology at the expense of personal interaction, and extended families tend to no longer live close together in our more mobile society.

The BYU researchers concluded that a lack of meaningful social relationships has the equivalent effects of smoking 15 cigarettes a day or being an alcoholic, is more harmful than not exercising, and is twice as harmful as obesity.

The consensus is that healthy relationships lower the production of stress hormones. It is also believed that when we have others who count on us, we feel an obligation, whether consciously or subconsciously, to be there for them when needed. Whatever the mechanism, healthy relationships yield longevity and quality of life and deserve to be a key factor in a successful retirement.

But what is a healthy relationship? I contend it has several components, all which are important. One is spending real face-to-face personal time with friends and family. This is not a facebook, email, twitter, texting thing. All of those are just fine when needed, but not at the expense of real-time in-person connections. Have you been to a restaurant lately and the family of four at the table nearby are all focused on their devices rather than on each other?

Second is being a part of networks (notice the plural) that have a social component. For example, my high school class continues to stay close, has mini-reunions around the country whenever possible, and gets together frequently as a hometown contingent. Do you belong to a group at your church, synagogue, or mosque? If you have retired, do you still get together with former teammates or colleagues? Do you have a hobby group, people who have common interests with each other and with you?

Finally, and integrated with the other two, are your two-o'clock-in-the-morning-friends. These are the people in your life who you would have no qualms calling in the middle of the night to ask for help and know that, without hesitation or question, your friend would be on the way. And they would similarly rely on you with a middle-of-the-night call. These are the friends or family members who are closest to you and who are most crucial in affecting your mental and physical health.

One could extrapolate from available research that having at least seven people with whom you have this level of relationship is a sweet spot. For those who do have this number, it is hard to relate to those who don't. Yet, when I ask retirement life-planning workshop attendees to share how many 2:00am friends they have, it is not uncommon for the vast majority to have three or fewer.

The other point to make here relates to a difference on this key element by gender. In general, and I emphasize that—in general, men have a more difficult time establishing closer personal relationships, especially outside the workplace. If you are male, you may need to and want to spend time focusing on this key element.

Do you have a number of 2:00am friends and family who you frequently spend time with and networks of social groups that surround you? Importantly, if you are still working, can you project that you will have these when you retire? Your answers will likely affect your longevity and quality of life.

> HEALTHY RELATIONSHIPS ASSESSMENT: Candidly assess yourself on the 1-to-5 scale for the following statement:
> <u>If not yet retired,</u>
> **I am confident that in retirement, I will have a meaningful number of 2:00am friends, will visit frequently with friends and family, and will be involved in several social networks.**
>
> <u>If already retired</u>
> **I have a meaningful number of 2:00am friends, visit frequently with friends and family, and am involved in several social networks.**
>
> Assessment Rating: _____

Key Element #7
Growth

"Growth itself contains the germ of happiness."
Pearl S. Buck

"Intellectual growth should commence at birth and cease only at death."
Albert Einstein

No, this is not about growth of your waistline when, as an elite athlete, you move on from your year-round training regimen. And it is not about growing your investment portfolio or your list of 2:00am friends, although those are important. It is about intellectual growth.

This is the one key element that takes a different direction for the two generations of retirees, young elite athletes and older career-oriented non-athletes. For the elite athlete, growth is figuring out what his or her second career will be and seeking the knowledge and skills required to succeed. For the career-oriented non-athlete professional, growth is focused on replacing the intellectual stimulation that his or her career delivered on a daily basis.

Elite Athletes

A great number of college student-athletes take the "student" part of the title seriously. For those who do, they are in a similar position as their non-athlete peers to graduate and move on to their planned careers, as did Dan Batsch, the University of Wisconsin football player you met earlier, who completed his engineering degree and built a successful career.

At issue, however, is that there are also a great number of student-athletes who pay little or no attention to the "student" part.

The good news is that the NCAA, which tracks graduation rates of its student-athletes, has been able to report consistently improving trends and record percentages. The bad news is that academics outside the NCAA have parsed the data and found there are still significant concerns. For example, elite athletes in the two major sports, basketball and football, graduate at significantly lower rates than do those in the general student population. The uncertain news is whether those student-athletes who do earn diplomas do so with a degree that puts them in good stead to pursue a meaningful career.

When John Thompson was coaching the Georgetown Hoyas, he kept a deflated basketball in his office to remind students that they needed to do well academically to prepare for life-after-basketball. He would say, "Winning is important. Playing the game is very important. But a man is measured not by what his arms can do but by his brains. You have to be able to do other things."

If you are an elite athlete who is not prepared for a career when you leave college or if you are among that small percentage who goes on to and retires from professional sports or the Olympics, your success will, in large part, be driven by new learning. Once you decide what you want to do with your life, it is likely that you will need to build new skills and knowledge to enable you to successfully change direction.

Some examples of growth for elite athletes:

➢ Garrett Broshuis, who retired from a six-year minor league pitching career, went to law school, and is now a practicing attorney.

➢ NBA player, Jabari Walker, left Duke University after one season to enter the professional draft. He plans to return to Duke each summer to earn his degree, "I have dreams after basketball. I want to be a history teacher…I just want to give a piece of my knowledge to these kids one day."

➢ Tennis superstar, Venus Williams, earned her associate degree in fashion design and has a goal of getting an MBA, both degrees to help her focus on her design firm, V Starr Interiors.

➢ Upon leaving Louisiana State University after three years, NBA legend Shaquille O'Neal promised his mother he would return to his studies and complete a bachelor's degree. He met his commitment and continued to demonstrate his valuing of education, as he has gone on to earn his MBA and his Ed.D.

➢ Emmett Johnson played professional football in both the U. S. and Canada. In retirement, he has been an insurance agent, branch manager, and founder of his own agency. Johnson says, "You have to constantly expand your knowledge and experience...I take continuing education classes to maintain my license. I also obtained a Life Underwriter Training Council Fellow designation and am working on the Certified Insurance Counselor designation."

There are resources that can help you plan for and take the steps to enter a successful second career. Among them are programs at universities. And there is a rigorous program in Jacksonville, Florida called ONECOR924, whose mission it is "to educate, coach and train elite collegiate and professional athletes to successfully transition into professional roles."

Older Non-Athlete Professionals

As I was preparing for retirement and interviewing those who had already made the leap, one of the questions I asked was, "What has surprised you about retirement?"

Although they articulated it in different ways, virtually everyone I talked to said something like, "I've found it difficult to replace the intellectual stimulation I got from work."

Keeping mentally active is critical as we transition into and age through retirement. We are inundated with information about the value of keeping the mind active, and unfortunately, most of us know someone who is dealing or has dealt with dementia, either personally or as a caregiver.

"Use it or lose it" is but one of the reasons growth is key to a successful retirement. It is all too easy to find ourselves settling into a very small comfort zone. Yet, what if instead of limiting our activities to what we are comfortable with, we use our new-found freedom to stretch ourselves? What if we engaged in new, exciting activities instead of passively sitting in front of the television or social media?

There is nothing wrong with either of those, unless they dominate your time. Think about all of the wonderful things you could do with that time. Those who take full advantage of growth are those who are actively looking for new opportunities to get involved. And just as it is important for your attitude, being predisposed to say "yes" to opportunities will enhance growth as well.

The things you can do to stimulate your brain and get you fully engaged in life can be big things. Take a class at a local community college. Get involved in a new volunteer project. Design your own web site. Learn a new language. Join a discussion group. Travel to a place you have never been before, a place very different from other trips you have taken.

Or they can be small things. The next time you drive to the grocery store, take a different route than you normally do. Brush your teeth with the opposite hand (seriously, try it). Eat dessert first. Listen to different music and read different genres. Instead of ordering from the menu at a restaurant, just tell the waitperson, "Feed me."

Expand your comfort zone. Keep your mind active and sharp. Enjoy new and different opportunities. Use it or lose it. As my friend, Keith, tells attendees during our retirement life-planning workshops, "The only difference between a rut and a grave are the dimensions." Morbid? Yes. Instructive? Also yes.

GROWTH ASSESSMENT: Candidly assess yourself on the 1-to-5 scale for the following statement:

If an elite athlete

I have a learning plan in place and am taking the steps to prepare for a successful life after my athletic career ends.

If a career-oriented non-athlete

I fill my life with a diverse list of new and challenging activities that keep me intellectually stimulated, and I am constantly looking for opportunities to take me out of my comfort zone.

Assessment Rating: _____

Key Element #8
Fun

"Laughter is the shortest distance between two people."
Victor Borge

"Just play. Have fun. Enjoy the game."
Michael Jordan

It's September. You are in the 151st game of your 12th MLB season. Your team is out of the playoff picture and you are down 7-2 in the sixth inning. You reported for spring training in early February after having worked out all winter to stay in playing shape. You have been playing every day but dealing with a blister on your throwing hand, another on your right foot, and chronic elbow pain. Are you having fun yet?

It's early April. You have been a CPA, running your own small firm, for most of your 62 years. You've been working your typical 12-hour days, seven days a week during tax season. Your grandson's third birthday is coming up, and you will probably miss the party, because an important and impatient client just called and told you all of the numbers are changing. You have a persistent headache, and the arthritis in your hip is acting up. Are you having fun yet?

Okay, I get it, if your career is something you love to do, it can be fun...at times. This may be especially true for elite athletes, for whom the general consensus is that one of the things that separates them from the masses of really-good athletes is their love of the game and the just plain fun they have playing it.

Regardless of whether you view your career as fun or not, the key questions looking forward are a) do you know how to build fun into your retirement, and b) will you?

It is noncontroversial that fun has health benefits. It is a de-stressor. Frequently, fun comes from being active, playing, being with friends, pursuing passions—all of which have health benefits of their own.

Did you know that children laugh an average of 300 to 400 times each day, while adults laugh an average of only ten to 15 times? Having fun triggers laughter, which has consistently been shown to be therapeutic. It improves the body's immune system, helps stave off the physical and emotional characteristics of stress, has a positive effect on blood pressure and heart function, and it decreases pain. Socially, laughter strengthens relationships, helps reduce conflict, and promotes group bonding. "Laughter is the best medicine."

You can plan fun into your life, or you can take advantage of being spontaneous. Ann and I have fun planning our vacations, then enjoying what we planned. My sister and brother-in-law, Marti and Harvey approach vacations much differently. "Where are you going on vacation?" Their reply, usually pointing in the same direction, "That way."

I'll stop now. I don't think I really have to convince you that having fun is good for you. Just do it! Envision creating a retirement that includes things that are just plain fun to do, whether planned or spontaneous.

FUN ASSESSMENT: Candidly assess yourself on the 1-to-5 scale for the following statement:

<u>If not yet retired</u>

I can envision having a retirement life full of activities that are just plain fun to do.

<u>If already retired</u>

I have many activities in my life that are just plain fun to do.

Assessment Rating: _____

Key Element #9
Well-Being

"You're in pretty good shape for the shape you are in."
Dr. Seuss

"And what is a man without energy? Nothing – nothing at all."
Mark Twain

What is well-being? The Centers for Disease Control and Prevention (CDC) states, "There is no consensus around a single definition of well-being, but there is general agreement that at minimum, well-being includes the presence of positive emotions and moods, the absence of negative emotions, satisfaction with life, fulfillment, and positive functioning. In simple terms, well-being can be described as judging life positively and feeling good."

That covers a very wide range. But guess what—so do the first eight key elements. Build a retirement game plan around the key elements, add a component of physical fitness, and in essence, you will have developed a solid well-being plan.

There's another way to think about pursuing a holistic approach to well-being. Tony Schwartz is a leading advocate for thinking about well-being as developing and sustaining "energy" in your life. He refers to what he calls "four core needs." They are physical energy, emotional energy, mental energy, and the energy of purpose. Sound familiar? Attitude, healthy relationships, growth, purpose, and the other key elements can and should be sources of energy.

The concept of energy has specific meaning in the context of a discussion about retirement. When we build our game plan to include the right daily habits and to include a broad portfolio of meaningful activities, we will not only have the energy we need at any given time, but we can expect that we will also have the energy to support what we want to do well into our futures. This concept applies to all retirees, but it plays out a bit differently for elite athletes and the older non-athletes.

If you are in your teens, 20s, or 30s and competing in a sport at the college level, professionally, or on an Olympics team, you are deeply rooted in a year-round training program, systematically designed to keep you in prime physical shape. Your daily habits keep you strong, flexible, aerobically fit, and functionally prepared for your sport. Your routine is designed to develop the energy you need for each individual game, meet, match, or tournament, but also to sustain you through the long season. What daily habits will you adopt when you retire to develop and sustain the energy you need to do what your game plan includes?

If you are in your 50s, 60s, or 70s and working in an all-consuming career, you may not be in the best of physical shape. Yet, hopefully, you have developed a routine to create the energy you need to be successful. What will your energy routine be when you retire? Will you benefit from having/taking the time to develop better fitness, nutrition, sleep, and other daily habits?

Ensuring you have the personal well-being, the energy, to live the retirement life you want, now and into your future, is critical to following your game plan.

WELL-BEING ASSESSMENT: Candidly assess yourself on the 1-to-5 scale for the following statement:

If not yet retired

I have a plan of daily habits and a portfolio of meaningful activities to ensure I have sufficient energy to do what I want to do in my retirement life and sustain that energy well into my future.

If already retired

I practice the daily habits and have a portfolio of meaningful activities in place to ensure I have sufficient energy to fully do what I want to do in my life and sustain that energy well into my future.

Assessment Rating: _____

Key Element #10
Game Plan

---

*"Planning is bringing the future into the present
so you can do something about it now."*
Alan Lakein

"Mistakes come from doing, but so does success."
John Wooden

So far, you have developed your knowledge about the retirement playing field, including understanding what the challenges are that you may face and the phases of retirement that you are likely to go through. You have begun to build your game plan by understanding the first nine key elements of a fulfilling retirement, and you have candidly assessed yourself on where you are in your life today relative to those key elements.

This final key element answers the question, "So what?" And it sets the stage for the remainder of the book, which will walk you through how to ensure you have the game plan that is right for you.

It is important that you have a game plan. You already know this. You would not expect to be successful at your sport or your business without one. With regards to a game plan for retirement, there are three considerations:

1. The plan is holistic.

2. The plan is written.

3. You have discussed the plan with those closest to you to get their thinking about it and to ensure they know how the plan will affect them.

The first consideration should be pretty obvious by now. To the extent you can incorporate all of the key elements in your life game plan, you will have the best odds of living the retirement you deserve. Make your plan "holistic."

The second consideration may not have occurred to you, but there is no controversy about whether writing your plan down will meaningfully increase your odds of actually doing it—some say by as much as five times.

Writing it down also serves to facilitate consideration number 3, discussing your plan with those closest to you. Retirement game plans are more successful when everyone on your team is on the same plan.

The bad news is that you likely do not have a written game plan you've discussed with those closest to you. The good news is that creating one is what we're about to work on together. So, assess yourself now for this key element, but you might want to revisit it after you go through the remaining chapters. Hopefully by then, you will have improved your assessment rating.

GAME PLAN ASSESSMENT: Candidly assess yourself on the 1-to-5 scale for the following statement:

Whether already retired or not

I have a holistic game plan for my retirement. It is written down, and I have discussed it with those closest to me.

Assessment Rating: _____

To get you ready for the next chapter, create a simple two-column table, either on paper or electronically. Label the first column "Key Element" and the second column "Assessment Rating." In the Key Element column, list the ten key elements, and next to each, put the Assessment Rating you gave it in second column.

Chapter 5

My Game Plan

---

*"It was OK when I retired from the game,
because I knew I had a plan."*
Marcus Lattimore

---

*"To be totally fulfilled, you have to find something that piques your interest
almost as much as playing the sport. You can't just sit back and do
nothing."*
Cal Ripken, Jr.

Don Davey
Professional Football Player
"victorious"

Only one person in the history of the NCAA has been an Academic All-American for four consecutive years. That would be Don Davey, when he was a defensive lineman at the University of Wisconsin, earning All-Big Ten and All-American honors as well as earning his Bachelors and Master's Degrees in Mechanical Engineering.

Don was a third-round draft pick and went on to play for the Green Bay Packers for four years before moving to the Jacksonville Jaguars during the team's inaugural year and helping lead them to an AFC Championship Game in only their second campaign. His career ended at age 29 during his seventh NFL season, when he tore an ACL in a Monday night game, and his knee was reconstructed the next day.

In both his football career and in his post-NFL phase of life (Don refers to it as his "transition" versus his "retirement"), he has been motivated by Vince Lombardi's statement, "...I firmly believe that any man's finest hour—

his greatest fulfillment to all he holds dear—is that moment when he has to work his heart out in a good cause and he's exhausted on the field of battle—victorious."

In that regard, Don may be the poster child for creating a full and fulfilling life after ending his career as a professional athlete. Since his retirement, Don, among other activities:

✓ Founded Disciplined Equity Management (DEM), an institutional money management firm, in which about 20% of his clients are current or former professional athletes.
✓ Is rearing and enjoying his five daughters with his wife, Kristen, who was his high school sweetheart.
✓ Owns 16 Firehouse Subs franchises in Wisconsin and the Orlando area—he is the largest single franchisee in the chain.
✓ Is a "Founding Member" of Trilogy Athletes, whose mission it is "to build a supportive community where forward-thinking professional athletes and Olympians gather to discover and access the best ideas available to transition successfully to life after sport."
✓ Owns Parrothead Properties, a real estate investment company with commercial and residential holdings in Florida and Wisconsin.
✓ Volunteers with multiple charities, including Give Kids the World, Memories with Love, the Tom Coughlin Jay Fund, and the Rubick Run.
✓ Competes in both local and international triathlons and at age 46, reached a long-time goal of completing an Ironman World Championship in Hawaii.

We'll reconnect with Don in the next chapter, when he helps us think about putting together a winning retirement financial team.

Not every retired athlete needs to have a retirement game plan as full as Don's. But why not? And not every retired older non-athlete needs to have a retirement game plan as full as mine. But why not? Here is but part of my list:

✓ Author and marketer of six published books (five non-fiction; one novel) and working on book seven

✓ Management consultant, helping small and large non-profits around the country, with a focus on organizations in the cancer prevention and cure community, develop their strategic plans

✓ Cofounder of and partner in LifeScape Solutions, LLC in which *Your Retirement Quest* coauthor, Keith Lawrence, and I serve financial services firms and companies to help their clients and employees, respectively, plan for the non-financial aspects of retirement

✓ Baseball player in a local over-60 league and in tournaments in Florida and Cooperstown

✓ Web site designer for my personal author's site and a site dedicated to my high school class and their exceptional accomplishments

✓ Blogger on retirement-relevant issues on three different sites

✓ Community volunteer and non-profit board member

✓ Gym rat, working out for a couple of hours, four days each week

✓ Active grandfather of four

✓ Extensive traveler with my wife, Ann

Just like fingerprints, everyone's retirement game plan will be different, customized for you based on your life circumstances, your background, your interests, and your key element assessment. The intent of this chapter is to provide you with a framework and several tools that you can use to develop your personalized plan.

These planning tools are either directly built on the key elements, or they complement the key elements but have their own basis for being helpful.

A point to make before we go on. It is not my intention to suggest that you spend an inordinate amount of time doing the planning. I am sure you will find that each of these tools will be helpful, but they will also be straightforward. In that regard, I suggest that you not think of these as a list of tools from which to choose just one, but rather as a tool kit where each of them can serve a purpose for you.

Planning Tool #1
Bucket List

You may have seen the 2007 movie, *The Bucket List*, with Morgan Freeman and Jack Nicholson, in which each has a terminal illness and jointly creates and sets out to complete their bucket list, those things they want to do in their lives in the time they have left. The concept of a bucket list is powerful, but I would propose two changes relative to the movie.

1. For most of us, thankfully, use of the bucket list is not about making our list of things we want to in the little time we have left. Think of your bucket list as things you would be excited about looking forward to doing, about planning to do, about actually doing, about relating to others, and about reminiscing afterwards. As the lyrics of the Tim McGraw song say, "I hope you get the chance to live like you were dyin'."

2. Most think of bucket list items as the big dreams, like traveling to Australia/New Zealand, writing that novel, or hiking the Appalachian Trail. And the big dreams are great and should be included. But the items can be smaller as well, like going to the new neighborhood restaurant, seeing a live performance of *Porgy and Bess*, teaching your granddaughter to play gin, or visiting each of the county parks in your area.

Sit down with a pen and paper or at your computer, and without making any judgement about whether you will actually be able to pull them off, just begin writing items on your list. Yes, there is that concept of writing it down again. You are more likely to pay attention to and do the list if you write it down versus just having it in your head.

You will find that just creating the list is energizing and that once you have it, you will be adding to it as you come across new ideas. If you need some help, ask friends what's on their bucket list. First of all, they will likely have thought of some good ideas you had not thought of, and second, you will likely find some things that would be fun to do with them.

When you complete an item, physically check it off or cross it out. Some people move their completed items to a separate list.

There are other approaches that meet the need, because the principles are the same. For example, a woman at one of my retirement life-planning workshops told me, "I don't have a bucket list; I have bucket jars." She has three jars on a counter, one labeled "Places to Go," one labeled "Activities and Games," and one labeled "Let's Eat." When she gets a bucket jar idea, she takes a small piece of paper, writes her idea, and puts it in the appropriate jar. She frequently dumps the contents of a jar on the counter, checks the paper notes, and picks something to begin planning.

Figure out what works for you, but create a written bucket list and keep it active, both doing the items and adding to the list. Experience is that the bucket list is a good way to get the planning juices flowing, so after reading the rest of this chapter, you may want to consider using this tool first. Or better yet, take a quick break and start writing—you'll be surprised how many items you'll generate in a short time. Remember-no judgement. Just write!

Planning Tool #2
Start/Stop/Continue

Are you back from your bucket list? Feel free to take a moment to add other items to it as you think of them.

This next tool is the first one based on the key elements, and it can be considered as the core of game planning. Create a simple three-column chart, again either electronically or on paper. Label the first column "Key Elements" and write them in. Column two is "Rating Assessment"—simply transfer your ratings to this column for each of the key elements. Label the third column "Start/Stop/Continue," and leave the most room in this one for writing.

Here is how to use the Start/Stop/Continue tool. For key elements with a low rating, like a 1 or a 2, it is likely that one or both of two things are true. There are things missing from your life that if you begin to do them, they will enhance that key element. This would mean that there are likely things that you should "start" to do.

It is also a possibility that there are things that exist in your life today that are getting in the way of enhancing that key element. These are barriers and things you should "stop" in your life.

I'll provide you with some typical examples of "start" and "stop" items shortly.

For those key elements you have rated for yourself as being a 4 or a 5, there may certainly still be some "start" or "stop" actions. But since these are doing well, it is more likely that these will yield things in your life that you want to "continue." It will be valuable to take the time to acknowledge what you are doing that is working well and writing these things down. First, it will just feel good to do that. Second, if in the future, you find yourself struggling with a key element that had not been an issue for you before, returning to the list of "continue" items may prompt you to realize that you had, in fact, not continued something that was making a positive difference for you.

If you have key elements rated 3, it is likely that they will have more of a mixture of "start," "stop," and "continue" items.

Four points before we look at some examples:

1. Pick one key element to work on to get started. Most of the time, it is best if you pick one you have rated a 1 or 2. Spend some time with that one key element, then when you feel comfortable that you're getting the hang of creating your "start/stop/continue" items, move on to work on the other key elements. Remember, be holistic by eventually (sooner better than later) bringing all of the elements into your life.

2. Be mindful not to create a long list, especially "start" items. You'll want to create a plan that is doable, so you don't get discouraged. As you are creating your list, set some priorities as you go—maybe even focusing on only one or two things to get started. When you have successfully brought the first priority items into your life, you can consider adding new priorities.

3. Apply leverage across key elements. Even though you will initially work with each of the key elements separately, you'll soon realize that some things, perhaps most things, you are including will have a positive effect on other key elements as well. One great example we frequently see goes like this.

The game planner has a low rating in Giving Back and includes a plan item that is something like, "Talk to the social action chairperson at church to find out what volunteer opportunities might interest me."

Our planner realizes that this action step is also helping Healthy Relationships, because it gets her involved with a network of like-minded people, who she now frequently interacts with. And she realizes that the action has made a positive impact on Passions, because one of the volunteer opportunities is helping tutor young students at a local disadvantaged school, and the work sparks her passion for children.

Can you also see how this new activity can trigger positive effects on Growth, Fun, Well-Being, and/or Attitude? Selecting the right actions for one key element can make a difference in many. And aren't those the actions you would prefer doing?

4. Make your plans doable by taking one step at a time. For example, you might be a 65-year old about to retire, and you haven't spent any time for the past 20 years exercising. If you rated yourself low on Well-Being, and you probably should have, then you may want to work on getting fit. But your "start" item should not be, "Get fit."

That isn't actionable. Rather your "start" item might be, "Join the local gym and talk to a personal trainer to figure out how to effectively get started." Or it might be, "Take a walk in the neighborhood for 20 minutes at least four times per week."

Once you complete your first "start" task, you can determine what your next one should be toward the eventual aim of getting fit. This point also speaks to the fact that your plan will be dynamic, constantly changing to fit what you've accomplished and your changing life circumstances. We'll talk more about this in Planning Tool #5, Game Plan Adjustments, later in this chapter and in even more detail in Chapter 9.

Some Examples (just to give you a flavor of what your items might look like):
➢ Start:
  o Game Plan: Create a first draft of my written bucket list.

Alan Spector

- o Financial Security: Talk to friends to find out who are the financial advisors they are using and why, and create an A-List of advisors to interview.
- o Healthy Relationships: Join my high school reunion planning committee.
- o Healthy Relationships: Call my out-of-town sister at least once a week.
- o Growth: Design my own family web site.
- o Giving Back: Talk to the social action chairperson at church to find out what volunteer opportunities might interest me.
- o Passions: Talk to the local garden shop about how to get started on that garden I've been wanting to create in the back of the house.
- o Life Purpose: Use the Franklin/Covey Mission Statement Builder to see what it tells me.

➢ Stop:
- o Well-Being: Drinking soda.
- o Attitude: Spending so much time with that friend who does nothing but complain.
- o Giving Back: Watching half of my current amount of TV (inference: replace it with a Giving Back project or a Growth project or pursuing a hobby that matches your Passions or spending time with friends to build Healthy Relationships)
- o Financial Security: Playing the lottery

➢ Continue:
- o Life Purpose: Going to the church study group I belong to that meets twice a month.
- o Passions: Going to the annual custom car show that comes to town.
- o Game Plan: Checking my plan every three months to make sure it is still working.
- o Attitude: Writing in my gratitude journal every night before I go to bed.
- o Healthy Relationships: Having the whole family over for dinner every other Sunday.

96

- o   Growth: Planning a vacation to a new place every year.
- o   Financial Security: Reviewing my financial plan with my advisor every three months.

The examples above would work for either generation of retirees. There may be game plan items that are generation specific, but what is most important is that you think about your "start/stop/continue" plan in the context of your personal life circumstances. What will enhance your personal game plan, raise your lower key element assessment ratings, and sustain your higher ratings?

Planning Tool #3
Critical Decision Making

There are critical decisions that many retirees face that can be better made by using the key elements. Here are three that are common, and you may have others.

1.   Where will I live, and in what kind of home will I live?
   - ➤   The retiring elite athlete may have lived in one or more locations growing up, gone to school in another, trained in another, and played in many. The athlete may also be building a young family with changing housing needs.
   - ➤   The older retiree may have relocated several times as part of his or her career and has been considering warmer climes, downsizing now that the kids are out of the house, finding a small place in the mountains as a second home, or whether a house, condo, or apartment would work best.
2.   Should I work in retirement, and if so, what work should I do?
   - ➤   The retiring athlete may be leaving college and looking for work, may need to supplement his or her professional income, or may have amassed a significant nest egg from his or her professional career. The athlete is likely looking forward to many decades during which to find a meaningful life direction.

97

> ➤ The older retiree knows that his or her skills and experiences can benefit other organizations and has the energy to help, has a good business idea he or she wants to make work in a marketplace, and knows there are benefits to continuing to do some level of work in retirement.

3. Which of the many opportunities coming my way should I decide to do, defer, or not do?

> ➤ The retiring athlete's name recognition, perhaps nationally or at least in his or her local community, could at least for a time, create a number of opportunities. And if athletes have spent time planning for and practicing retirement, they have a list of things they want to do and are always looking for other opportunities. (more about practicing retirement in Chapter 7)

> ➤ Older retirees know their retirement will be enhanced if they look for opportunities to bring meaningful activities into their lives. If they have spent time planning for and practicing retirement, they already have a portfolio of meaningful things they want to do as they transition into retirement. It is not uncommon for those who have planned and practiced to be in a position to say, "I have so much going on, I don't know how I had the time to work!"

Here is an example of one couple who would have benefited by using the key elements to help with a decision. Even before they retired, Barbara and Jim had decided that they wanted to get out of their cold Midwestern big city. Immediately upon retiring, they sold the old home, bought one in Florida, and moved. The purchase and move solved their growing dislike for winter weather, but it didn't take long for other issues to show up.

Their close friends and immediate family were "back home." They had been prominent community volunteers and found it difficult to replace that in their lives in their new community. It was even difficult to find new doctors and dentists, get comfortable in a new church, replace barbers, hairdressers, the handyman, and so many other connections and services.

And finally, they found the cost of the move and a higher cost of living was draining their resources.

Within a year of moving, they decided to move "back home."

The attraction of warm weather had been a unidimensional way to make their decision to move to Florida. Their decision was not holistic. What if they had considered all of the key elements of a fulfilling retirement up front? They may have determined early that they were negatively affecting the key elements of "healthy relationships," "giving back," and "financial security," and perhaps others.

Does it seem obvious to you that they should have thought of all these things in the first place? You'd be surprised. In that regard, here is a critical decision making tool. It will not make decisions for you, but it will give you some insights you might not have otherwise had.

Time for another chart. The first column is labeled "Key Elements," and the second is "Assessment Rating." There will be additional columns, the number being determine by how many options you want to consider in the decision you are trying to make; each column labelled to reflect a different option.

To use the chart to your advantage, follow these steps:

1. Be clear on what decision you're trying to make. For our couple, they are asking the question, "Where will we live, and in what kind of home?"

2. Figure out all the options you want to consider and write each as a heading in its own column. For our couple, this might be their list of options:
   - Option A: Stay in our current home full time, and travel to Florida once or twice each winter for a couple of weeks each.
   - Option B: Live in our current home during the spring, summer, and fall; buy a condo in Florida and spend the winter there.
   - Option C: Same as Option B, but also downsize to a condo in our home town.
   - Option D: Move to Florida full time.

3. Write the rating from your most recent assessment for each key element. This will give you a frame of reference as you see key elements either positively or negatively affected by a given option.

4. For each option column, go down the list of key elements and assess each one for how that option will affect it—positively, negatively, or not at all.

If the option will positively affect a key element, put a "+" sign in that block. If the option will negatively affect a key element, put a "-" sign in that block. If you conclude there is no effect, leave the block for that key element blank. For our couple, they would have had "-" signs in the Financial Security, Giving Back, and Healthy Relationships blocks, and perhaps others in the full-time-in-Florida option. The chart would have at least given them reason to pause and consider another option.

5. When you've completed the key elements for each option, you will see in front of you a map of your decision. Some columns, the good options, will have lots of "+" signs, and the bad options will have fewer "+" signs and more "-" signs.

This tool will not make the decision for you, but it will give you some guidance and cause you to mull over the various things you might not have otherwise thought of. Remember the word, "holistic?" In our context, it is when you bring all of the key elements into your life, which is exactly what this tool helps you do.

Follow the process for any decision you need to make that has options available to you. In fact, it also works for a "yes/no" decision. What if you are an elite athlete who has accumulated a significant nest egg through your career? A friend proposes an opportunity to you—invest in his new restaurant or franchise or whatever. You want to help, but you say, "Give me some time to think about it."

Pull out your key element critical decision making chart.

Step 1: The question is "Will I invest?"
Step 2: Write the heading for your option in its column, "Yes-Invest."
Step 3: Enter your assessment ratings.
Step 4: For each key element, mark a "+" or a "-" in each block or leave it blank. Maybe you would have a positive mark for Healthy Relationships (you are helping a close friend) and Growth (you have never done anything like this before and learning the business would be a growth opportunity). Maybe you would have a negative for Passion (you don't really care about that business), Financial Security (your trusted, expert

advisors say that it is a very risky investment), Giving Back (it will take time away from a volunteer project you have been wanting to do), and Life Purpose (your purpose is making a difference in the lives of children, but this investment has no connection to that).

Step 5: Look at your distribution of pluses and minuses. This should help you make the decision, or at least raise some questions you might not have otherwise thought about. You've positioned yourself to make a holistic decision.

Critical decision making—it's a worthwhile tool—use it.

Planning Tool #4
Finding the Magic

One way to think about choosing what you may want in your life's portfolio of meaningful activities is to "find the magic" using this tool. Here's the concept—if you know what you're passionate about, those things you love to do; and you know what your strengths are, those things you are great at and have experience with; and you know what the world needs, those things where you can make a difference; then bring them all together, and you will "find the magic."

Brett Favre is obviously passionate about football; he profoundly understands and can teach offensive technique and strategy; and there was a need at a local high school for an offensive coordinator. Magic!

When Judy Van Ginkel retired, she brought together her passion for children, children's health, and her Cincinnati community; her abilities to bring people together in common cause; and the dire need for at-risk families having their first child to receive the guidance they need to help those children be healthy and school ready. Judy founded Every Child Succeeds, and as of this writing, she is in her early 70's and still leading the organization. Magic!

Olympic judo gold medalist, Kayla Harrison has established the Fearless Foundation. Kayla revealed that she had been a victim of sexual abuse and has a passion for helping other victims through the foundation's mission, "to shine a light on the darkness that is child sexual abuse and to enrich the lives of survivors through education and sport." Through Kayla's judo mastery, the foundation has a health and wellness program to help increase survivor self-confidence. Magic!

Baby Boomer Elaine Unell is passionate about creativity and has skills and experience across a wide range of artistic genres. In retirement, her passion for and skill in creating unique pottery pieces have grown exponentially. She creates for her own satisfaction, and others are eager to purchase her creations, including yours truly. Magic!

Chris Herren played his college basketball at Boston College and Fresno State at a level that led to his being picked 33rd overall in the 1999 draft. His stay in the NBA was brief, and he played for several years overseas. At issue was his drug use. Felonies, an overdose, and intensive rehab led him to a passion to help others avoid what he went through. Chris has the speaking skills to inspire the young people he addresses around the country, and he has created The Herren Project to facilitate his personal mission. Magic!

Jill Chapin is passionate about books and how they can fire up a child's curiosity. After she retired, she began reading to children at the local elementary school and employed her skill of using different voices and inflections to keep their attention. She knew she was making a difference when a seven-year-old drew a picture of her reading to the class. Hovering over Chapin in the picture is a stick figure with a halo over its head saying, "You are so coming up here." Magic!

What are you passionate about—what do you love to do?

What are your strengths—what are you great at; what have you experienced?

What does the world, your local community, your family, your friends need?

Answer these questions, then act. Magic!

Planning Tool #5
Ideal Day/Week/Year

You can use this tool on its own or, and I'd suggest this, you can use it after first getting some experience with tools one through four. The purpose of Tool #5 is two-fold: 1) to help address the loss of the structure your career provided you, and 2) to provide an additional planning target to strive for, creating the retirement you want it to be and helping you figure out how you want to best spend the most important thing you have—your time.

Recall that during your career, one of the things that just shows up for you each day is structure, a schedule and a to-do list. A given daily athletic timetable might include practice time, film sessions, strength training, a game, interviews, and/or travel. The older generation's agenda might include patient or class schedules, meetings, presentations, phone calls, and/or travel. Retirement day comes, and the next day, all of that structure is gone. That can be a real opportunity; enjoying the freedom it provides. It can also be a significant issue.

Here's how the tool works. Address the ideal day first. Envision your retirement. Think about the exciting activities you've included in your plans from the first four tools. Now, picture this—you wake up to a day of retirement and you know it's going to be an ideal day.

As you've become accustomed, it's time to write it down—create a two-column table, labeling the first "Time" and the second "Activity." In the first column, list times in half-hour increments, starting with when you would like to wake up for your ideal day and ending when you would like to go to sleep.

The Activity column is where you enter how you would prefer to ideally spend those half-hour time slots. You can adjust timing by combining rows in the table. For example, if your ideal day includes a workout from 8:30 to 9:30, merge the 8:30 and 9:00 rows. If it would work best for you, create one table for an ideal weekday and another for an ideal weekend day.

You can break the chart up into time blocks that work best for you. Although I've seen some that get down to every-15-minute slots, I'd recommend a more general approach, at least to start. The ideal day exercise is simply intended to give you a benchmark to which you can compare your days as they are really unfolding. Making the comparison can help you strive to move your life toward your ideal.

A typical non-ideal day may be filled with watching television and monitoring social media. Those can be enjoyable activities, but they are passive and not as fulfilling as building activities on the ten key elements.

I've filled in my ideal day as an example only to help get your thinking started. It is not intended to indicate that mine is right for you. It is not. As we've said, retirement game plans are like fingerprints—they are unique to each of us as individuals.

Time	Activities
6:30 am	Wake up and Breakfast with Newspaper Puzzle Page
7:30	Research and Reading
9:00	Writing—Book and/or Blog
12:30 pm	Lunch with Crossword Puzzle
1:30	Volunteer Activities
3:30	Business Activities (Calls, Prep) or more Writing
5:30	Dinner with Ann
6:30	Play Baseball Game
10:30	Sleep

Once you have completed your ideal day chart, it's time to move on to your ideal week chart. Simply have a first column titled "Time" and subsequent headings for the days of the week. As for the ideal day chart, merge rows to accommodate activities longer than a half hour.

The ideal week exercise is the opportunity to build in those ideal activities that you would not necessarily want to do every day, either because you wouldn't have the time, or perhaps, they are things that just don't happen that often. Spreading your schedule out over a full week also allows you to include things that were vying for space in your ideal day but didn't make the cut. In my example, I want to research/write every day, but four days of working out is sufficient. I want to spend meaningful time with family (which includes grandchildren as often as possible) and friends, but not in the same way or at the same time every day. My weekly ideal helps me think about that and do the planning to create my real weekly schedule.

It is not my intent, nor should it be yours, to force fit the ideal schedule every day of every week. Rather, treat it as guidance. As you plan your actual schedule, which will change from week to week, move toward ideal, but don't become obsessive about it—that wouldn't be fun.

Your Ideal Year Chart can simply have 12 columns, each for a month of the year. Here are a few sample items that are on my chart for several of the months.

> ➤ January: Play Florida baseball tournament
> ➤ March through May: Conduct Retirement life planning workshops; Strategic Planning consulting engagement
> ➤ April: Major trip
> ➤ May through August: Play in local baseball league
> ➤ August: Join East Coast relatives on Jersey Shore
> ➤ December: Kids and Grandkids all together for vacation
> ➤ Throughout the Year: Holiday celebrations

This part of the exercise enables you to build in things like vacation travel. Ann and I plan our travel about a year ahead to make sure of our priorities, our trips on the calendar so as not to double-book, and we're able to plan with others who will be affected by the schedule.

This is also when you can build in longer term planning activities like taking classes, signing up for entertainment venue series, planning larger home improvement projects, and other things that benefit from building them into schedules early.

Simply list the longer-term ideal activities in each month you would target to make them happen—again recognizing that this is a general target, not the actual scheduling activity.

The "Ideal" tool, for day, month, and year, can and should provide you with structure as you transition to and through retirement and prompt your thinking about what you need to do to move from what might be your typical un-planned day to your ideal day.

Planning Tool #6
Game Plan Adjustments

Ever-changing circumstances, some positive and some negative, are the rule in your career. When the circumstances change, you at least reconsider your game plan and perhaps change it.

➤ Your projected starting pitcher contracts food poisoning the day before game six of the World Series.

➤ You just received the judge's ruling that the new product you were about to launch does, in fact, violate your key competitor's patent.

➤ The gale-force winds that plagued the first two rounds of the British Open have died down prior to your round three tee time.

➤ You had planned to move on to the next subject in the curriculum, but virtually every one of your students did poorly on a test you were expecting them to pass with flying colors.

➤ The injury suffered by your high-scoring power forward has healed faster than anyone predicted, and she has been cleared to play in tomorrow night's game.

➤ You were ready to settle your lawsuit out of court, when you were pleasantly surprised by a new piece of evidence.

➤ You were expecting to be a third or fourth round pick in the NHL draft, but find yourself not having been selected.

➤ Your children told you that they were not interested in taking over the business that you founded and have put your heart and soul into for so many years.

I had a colleague who frequently reminded us, "A plan is only something from which to deviate." He did not mean ignore your plan. What he meant was that sticking to a plan in the face of new circumstances is folly.

That is why "Game Plan Adjustments" is a tool in our game-planning arsenal. Being explicit about the likelihood that we will be changing our plans as circumstances warrant will cause us to be open about that possibility; in fact, that probability.

Chapter 6

My Team

"I am a member of a team and I rely on the team...
the team, not the individual, is the ultimate champion."
Mia Hamm

"No matter whether you are a new or old team member,
you need time to adjust to one another."
Yao Ming

Did you know:

➤ it takes an NBA player an average of 21 games with a new team to recover his pre-transfer performance?

➤ nearly half of high-performing investment analysts don't replicate their pre-transfer performance with a new bank after five years?

Teams are important. But you already know that. The problem is that while we are still competing, we tend to think only about our sports team or our business team. We don't necessarily think about our retirement team. So let's do that.

Floorball is an indoor sport developed in Sweden in the 1960s and 1970s—five field players, a goalie, 40+ inch hockey-like sticks, a plastic ball with holes in it. There is an International Floorball Federation (IFF) and a movement to include the sport in the Olympics.

One of the things the IFF has done as part of its quest to enter the Olympics is declare its support of the expectations of the IOC's Entourage Commission, which includes this definition in its guidelines, "The Entourage comprises all the people associated with the athletes, including without limitation, managers, coaches, physical trainers, medical staff, scientists, sports organizations, sponsors, lawyers, and any person promoting the athlete's sporting career, including family members."

The IOC then shares a diagram that further expands the list of possible members of the athlete's entourage to friends, equipment service providers, sponsors, unions, agents; even spectators and governments.

By the way, the chairperson for the IOC Entourage Committee is Sergey Bubka, the Ukranian World Champion and Olympic gold-medalist pole vaulter.

Bottom line, whether in floorball, any other team sport, or in any individual sport, it takes a village to help an athlete be successful. While the team surrounding a collegiate student-athlete is not usually as extensive as that of the professional or Olympian, the concept is the same. Elite athletes at any level get accustomed to a broad base of support.

When an athlete moves from career into retirement, however, the support team, in large part, vanishes. Family and close friends may remain. Perhaps there is continued support from an agent, although a former NFL player told me that the agent "drops you like a hot rock."

The problem is no different for the older non-athlete who is retiring from a career, having been surrounded by a workplace support system, which may be comprised of boss, subordinates, colleagues, administrative staff, vendors, nurses, paralegals, specialists, unions, and on and on.

Who will your retirement team be, and why should you build one?

Why Build a New Team?

The value of being part of a team does not diminish as you move from the inevitability to the transition phase. In fact, your retirement team may be even more valuable. When you are playing, despite all of the support you are given, at the end of the day, you are the athlete. You provide the skills to deliver performance and be successful.

When you enter retirement, uncharted waters, you may do so without the knowledge, skills, and experience you need to be successful. In that regard, you become even more reliant on expert and caring support. You can certainly try to navigate on your own, but there are those who can help you create the retirement life you would like to live. At the very least, the right teammates can help get you to where you want to be more quickly than if you set out on your own.

I am assuming that creating a great retirement life and doing so quickly is exactly why you are reading this book. In that regard, you can count me in on your team already. Glad to be here.

There is another key reason your retirement team will be helpful that may not be as obvious. Earlier, we recognized that one of the things you lose when you retire is an accountability structure. During your career, you were driven to win. In fact, a meaningful part of what separates you from others has been your personal motivation to spend the time and energy needed to succeed. In many ways, you are self-motivated—you are a self-initiator!

You also know that you did well because there were others who helped you hold yourself accountable. As an athlete, you are accountable to your coach, teammates, and fans. As a non-athlete, you are accountable to your boss, shareholders, patients, clients, students, and colleagues.

None of us wants to fail ourselves, but we also don't want to fail those who are counting on us. Building the right retirement team includes those who will help you hold yourself accountable.

Let's look at who you might want to consider to be your retirement teammates. To do so, we'll investigate the two important components, your financial team and your life team. Both are critical, and they need to be integrated.

Financial Teammates

You met Don Davey, retired NFL defensive lineman, in the last chapter. Although he graduated from Wisconsin with a Master's in Mechanical Engineering, he took his post-football career in a different direction.

During his playing career, he had both personal experience and saw others having the same, with investment advisors who were not meeting client needs. Don used his engineering-based analytical skills to study the value of the advice he was being given and to develop techniques for managing his own money. His success led teammates to ask him for help.

The year he retired, Don founded his financial services firm, Disciplined Equity Management. His personal business experience, coupled with his financial acumen, has enabled him to successfully serve retired athletes and other high-net-worth clients. It also enables him to give us advice on building an effective retirement financial team, starting with two guiding principles.

➢ Select the individual professionals you need for their capability and integrity. We'll review shortly an approach to doing this. Here is a list of support professionals to consider for your team:
- o Financial advisor
- o Accountant
- o Estate Planning Attorney
- o Insurance Agent
- o Business Consultant

➢ Make sure you have one professional that coordinates your team in a way that makes sure each of your decisions has the best holistic (there's that word again) result. For Don's clients, he plays that role and uses two sports analogies and a business analogy to describe it:
- o This person is the "quarterback" who makes sure everyone on the team is using the same play book and is running the same play.
- o You are the "team owner," and you hire a "general manager" to build and coordinate the organization and the team toward the common objective of winning.
- o This is your personal "Chief Financial Officer," coordinating all of the financial aspects of your enterprise.

Finding the right financial services professionals, those who are capable of meeting your needs and who you can trust, is critical to building the right team. If you have a spouse or partner, involve them in the process. If not, recruit a family member or friend to help you think about these important selections.

1. Spend time with your spouse, partner, family member, or friend to determine what will be important to you as you seek out these support professionals. Write down that list. You should expect part of your list to be about their professional capability and some about how you feel about them, for example, their trustworthiness and whether their values seem to match yours. When Ann and I selected our financial advisor, who we have now been working with for 20 years, our final two candidates were both very capable. Yet they had very different business cultures—one felt much more corporate; the other more family-oriented. Family-oriented felt better to us, so we made that choice. I'm confident either would have worked out, but we've been pleased with both the results and the relationship of our choice for these many years.

2. If you are starting from scratch, begin with your choice of a financial advisor. This is the only person on your team whose financial incentive is tied to your financial success. It is likely this person will also be your "quarterback."

3. Create a list of candidates. One way to do this is to reach out to former players or colleagues you know who have been retired for a while and seem to be doing well. Ask them who they have chosen and why are they still using them.

4. Interview each candidate on your list A-list. Consider asking these questions:

    a. Have you worked with retired athletes before? If you are a non-athlete professional, ask if the interviewee has worked with others at your company or in your profession. Ask how long they have been in the financial services business, and ask for references.

    b. Describe your overall investment philosophy.

    c. What have your results been over the past ten years for clients in the range of my net worth? How does that compare to standard benchmarks?

    d. What is your experience with clients who are _____? Fill in the blank with what you may be thinking about doing in retirement. You may be getting involved with franchises or consulting or real estate or any number of things. You may be planning to focus on volunteering or creating a foundation. Formulate this question to make sure that the professional will understand the financial implications of your life choices.

e. Will I be working directly with you or will you pass me along to someone else in the firm? If someone else, who would that be? Talk to the person you will be working with. If this person is older, the good news may be that he or she is likely more experienced. The bad news may be that he or she may also be retiring soon—ask them about this.

f. Will you run a complimentary financial analysis for me to give me an idea of where I stand, to identify the issues I should be thinking about, and to give me an idea of how you would manage my money?

g. What are all of the fees that I will have, including your fees as my advisor and any fees associated with the investments you will be suggesting?

h. Do you have a list of other financial services professionals who you refer and work with to coordinate my account? Ask the interviewee to describe what they do to organize this team and how.

5. Either decide based on this first round of interviews, or if the interviews have prompted other questions, you may want to conduct a second session with each of the top two or three candidates and probe the additional areas.

This all may seem like an onerous process, but think about the implications of getting these choices either right or wrong.

The best time to establish your financial team is in the inevitability phase, while you are still playing or working. Working with your team can and should be an element of practicing retirement. If a financial team member is not performing to your expectations, either work with him or her to improve or change the team member. You should be fully satisfied with your team's professional capability and your relationship with them.

Life Teammates

Building your full retirement team is analogous to creating your game plan—finances are critical, but it's far from being all about the money. When you build your game plan, you need to build a plan that gives you financial security. But you also need a holistic life plan, one that brings all ten key elements of a fulfilling retirement into your life.

Similarly, when building your retirement team, a financial team is necessary, but it's far from being sufficient. The right team should be built to support all of the key aspects of your life.

Family Team

For many, the key to retirement success will lie in family relationships and how well you have involved family members in your game planning. There are some obvious family teammates to consider: spouse, partner, children, parents, siblings, and others who we have been close to over the years; for example, cousins, aunts, and uncles.

Those closest to you will be affected by your retirement, and your retirement will profoundly affect them. A great way to involve those closest to you is to initiate the "crucial conversations." Start these early in your game planning process.

Here are some crucial conversation topics and questions to get your thinking started. You'll note that most of these apply to both elite athletes and retiring non-athletes, but you'll also readily note that there are also some that are generation-specific. Not every crucial conversation will apply to your particular situation—pick the ones that are right for the person you're talking to. You'll prompt meaningful discussions that will lead to other important topics as well.

- ➤ Relationships
  - ○ What is the honest assessment of the state of our relationship?
  - ○ What steps can we take to make the relationship even better before retirement?
- ➤ Retirement Timing

- o When will I retire?
- o When will you retire?
- ➢ Retirement Game Plan
  - o What is my game plan? What is your game plan? What is our game plan?
  - o What is on my bucket list? What is on your bucket list? What is on our bucket list?
  - o Will either of us work in retirement? Doing what?
- ➢ Family Relationships
  - o What will our retirement relationship be with our parents, children, grandchildren?
  - o Will there be a financial commitment?
  - o Will there be a caregiving commitment?
- ➢ Planning Discussion
  - o With whom (e.g. children, family, friends) will we have a discussion about our retirement plans?
- ➢ Location
  - o Where will we retire? Which city? Which neighborhood?
  - o Will we have a second home? If so, where? How often would we go?
- ➢ Daily Routine
  - o What will our daily routine and other chores be when we're both home?
- ➢ Financial Plan
  - o What is our financial plan? Do we have a thorough and common understanding of it?
  - o Do we have the right financial advisor and full financial team?
  - o What do we need to do to make sure either of us could manage our finances if need be?
- ➢ Well-Being
  - o What steps should we be taking now to improve our health, fitness, and energy level to prepare for retirement?
- ➢ Practicing Retirement

- ○ What am I doing to practice retirement? What are you doing? What are we doing?
- ○ What other steps should we be taking to prepare for retirement?

One final point about crucial conversations—the discussion might be difficult, but if it is, that is a clear signal that it is necessary. And if it is difficult, it is also an indicator that life would be even more difficult if you did not have the conversation.

Personal Team

Others on your team can fill any one of a number of personal needs:

➢ <u>2:00am Friends</u>: One of the aspects of healthy relationships (key element #6) is having a number of 2:00am friends. These are the people in your life who you would have no qualms about calling in the middle of the night if you needed help, and you know that friend would, without hesitation, be on the way to help. And vice versa.

These are people you want on your team. Recall also that it is likely that only a limited number, if any, of these 2:00am retirement friends will be those who are your sports teammates or business colleagues. The research says the sweet spot is having seven or more, and they can be either family members or friends. For the sake of putting your retirement team together, think about being in the range of ten.

➢ <u>Clergy</u>: Certainly each of us has our own personal view of religion and in that regard, we also have our own personal view of what, if any, relationship we want or need with clergy. There are two reasons for including clergy on the list of possible positions on the team: 1) it might be right for you, and 2) this is one of those teammates that is worth considering when evaluating where to live. Some of your retirement teammates may be location-dependent. If you feel close to clergy in your current location and that is important to you, then this would be a consideration when making a living-location decision.

➢ <u>Accountability Partner(s)</u>: Making changes can be difficult. Yet, when you retire, so much is changing. Some changes are foist upon you. Others are choices you create as part of your retirement game plan. One way to think about helping you make a change in your life is to consider whether you have the skill, will, and support to make it.

o **Skill**: This is having the knowledge and capability to do the change. You may for example, want to go into broadcasting when you retire from your sport. But you may know little about the industry and have never actually been in front of a microphone in a broadcast setting. You would have some learning and skill building to do.

You may want to start gardening when you retire. Perhaps you are attracted to the idea, because you fondly recall being in the garden with your mother growing up, but know little about actually doing it yourself. You will want to develop the skill to get started. That will be enjoyable in itself—then more good news, continuing to develop even more skill contributes to the key elements "growth" and "fun."

o **Will**: This is having the motivation to change and doing two things to bring the change to life. First, take the initial step to making the change as quickly as possible. Second, sustain the new habit until it becomes part of your routine; some say that should be at least 21 days, but it is likely situational, based on the nature of the change and what works for you.

You may decide, for example, to increase your volunteering efforts with children. Take the first step as soon as you make this choice—for example, contact a volunteer coordinator at your local United Way to learn where you might be helpful. Then immediately contact that agency and schedule your volunteer time for the next three to four weeks. By then, you'll likely find it will have become part of your routine, and you'll be scheduling the coming weeks. If you put off making the contacts or doing the scheduling, you run the risk of never getting started.

A Baby Boomer friend decided to include a daily walking regimen in his well-being plan. When he made that choice, he took his first walk the next morning and continued to get out on the road every day for the next several weeks and has never looked back. He is now into his tenth year of taking a daily walk, regardless of the weather or where he is.

117

○ **Support**: This is having an accountability partner, someone you recruit to check in with you on how you are doing with any given change to help you hold yourself accountable in making that change. You may be able to handle some items on your own—great! But be honest with yourself—if you have any doubt, think about who you would want to help you make the changes in your life. This could be a single person, a support group, or a different person for each of the changes you're making. It might be one of your 2:00am friends.

This approach may sound onerous. To be clear, I'm not suggesting that your accountability partner is physically looking over your shoulder. It can be as simple as every time you see your partner, he or she asks you about the change you're making. An out-of-town friend of mine wanted to be more disciplined about his workout schedule. He asked me if I'd check how he was doing every time we talked on the phone, which is no more than once a month. When I agreed to this, he began emailing me with an update every week.

Another option that works is to be reciprocal accountability partners with someone. My wife and I go to the gym together four days a week. When we get there, she heads for Zumba classes, and I head for the aerobic equipment and weight room. It's pretty hard for either of us to tell ourselves that we don't feel like going on any given day, because the other one, our accountability partner, is getting ready and is at the door at the appointed time.

Well-Being Team

In your career as an elite athlete, you have been surrounded by fitness coaches, sports psychologists, trainers, team doctors, and anyone else needed to help keep you at a peak level of performance. In your career as a non-athlete professional, you may not have taken care of yourself the way you would have liked. For both generations, retirement will carry its well-being challenges and opportunities.

Athletes, how will you remain fit in a way that is in balance with the rest of your life? How will you deal with the wear and tear your body has undergone over the years?

Non-athletes, how will you use your new-found time to get into shape? How will you deal with the wear and tear your body has undergone as it has aged and continues to do so?

There are things you can figure out and do yourself. You can design and follow your own aerobics, strength, and flexibility regimen. You can design and follow your own nutrition regimen.

There are things you cannot figure out on your own, nor would you want to. Your team needs to have the right physicians, your personal doctor and dentist and specialists, if needed.

And there are things you may want help with, even though you might be able to do them on your own. Can a personal trainer help? How about a nutritionist? Okay, why not a masseuse?

The members of your well-being team are among those you need to consider when you are deciding where to locate in retirement. If you move to a new geography, you will need to build your new well-being team.

Retirement Team Roster

To complete the development of your retirement team, do this simple exercise on the next page. Well, actually using the chart is simple; filling in the right names might not be.

1. Determine whether you need someone in each of the listed "Positions" on your team. If you need the Position filled, write "Yes" in the "Need?" block. I've taken the liberty to let you know which I believe you'll need, but confirm those as well. You'll note that I didn't put a "Yes" in the blocks for "Spouse/Partner" or "Close Relative," not wanting to presuppose your personal life situation.

2. Scan the list of "Positions" to make sure that it is sufficient for you. If not, add "Others."

3. For each of the listed Positions for which you have answered "Need?" as "Yes," write in the name or names of the "Teammate(s)" who you want to fill each "Positions."

4. Establish a plan to recruit those "Teammate(s)." When the Position is filled, check the block in "Filled?" column.

Teams	Positions	Need?	Teammate(s)	Filled?
Financial Team	Financial Advisor	Yes		
	Accountant	Yes		
	Estate Planner	Yes		
	Insurance Agent	Yes		
	Business Advisor/Coach			
	Business Attorney			
Family Team	Spouse/Partner			
	Close Relative			
Personal Team	2:00am Friends	Yes		
	Clergy			
	Accountability Partner			
Well-Being Team	Personal Physician	Yes		
	Personal Trainer			
	Medical Specialist(s)			
	Dentist	Yes		
	Nutritionist			
Others				

You have your game plan and your team—time to practice.

Practicing

Before you actually play the game, whether you are entering an athletic contest or a business meeting, legal proceeding, medical operation, classroom lecture, or sales presentation, there are two additional aspects of preparation. The first is to practice, and the second is to recognize you are ready and commit yourself to winning.

Retirement is no different. You have understood the playing field, developed your game plan, and built your team. You know after years of experience that your success will, in large part, be based on whether and how well you have practiced. As Vince Lombardi said, "Practice does not make perfect. Only perfect practice makes perfect."

The next step is to ask yourself the questions, "Am I prepared to play? Have I put myself in a position to win?" If the answers are "Yes," then you can commit yourself to playing the game with confidence.

The two chapters in this section will cover why, when, and how to practice retirement and how to decide when you are ready to retire.

Chapter 7

Practicing Retirement

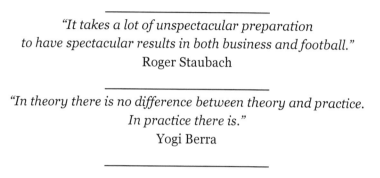

"It takes a lot of unspectacular preparation
to have spectacular results in both business and football."
Roger Staubach

"In theory there is no difference between theory and practice.
In practice there is."
Yogi Berra

Have you absorbed the Yogi-ism yet? I'll give you another moment. Okay, let's move on.

There may be no group of individuals who understands the concept of practicing better than elite athletes. Although there is some disagreement about the number, conventional wisdom has it that an athlete needs to put in at least 10,000 hours of practice to attain the performance level that can earn "elite" credentials.

Some argue the number is too high, and others argue it's too low, but the number doesn't really matter. It's the concept—we intuitively understand the value of practice. Staubach and Berra were right—so were the following:

"Practice puts brains in your muscle." Sam Snead

"The more I practice, the luckier I get." Arnold Palmer

"An ounce of practice is worth a ton of preaching." Mahatma Gandhi (No, he was not a cricket player. Look him up—we should all know who this man was and what he stood for.)

"My father taught me the only way you can make good at anything is to practice, and then practice some more." Pete Rose

Non-athlete professionals have also progressed through their careers by practicing. Doctors practice in medical school, during their internships, and during their residencies. Teachers have student teaching assignments. Pilots don't solo until they've spent untold hours with an instructor. Companies have extensive training programs.

If we know the value of practicing, then why not practice retirement?

Practicing during the Inevitability Phase

By now, you either have a written retirement game plan or have at least started working on it. Your plan is the foundation to begin practicing retirement, and doing so while you are still competing is the sweet spot. There should be activities on your game plan that you are looking forward to doing once you retire. Practicing means figuring out how to bring those activities into your life today.

Here's a simple chart to help. You can start by filling it out on the page, but you'll quickly find out that just as your retirement game plan will change over time, so will what you are practicing. So, you may want to create a hard copy or electronic version that will work best for you, both for filling it out and keeping it current.

Throughout the rest of this chapter, I'll be providing you with some thoughts about why you will want to practice and giving you some examples of what others have done to prompt your thinking. As the chapter goes on, you may want to create a list of the activities you have planned for retirement and how you are or will be practicing them now.

Although the value of the general concept is intuitive, there are some specific reasons you'll want to begin and continue practicing retirement.

1. Preparation—There may be some things you are planning to do in retirement for which you'll need to develop new knowledge and skills. Here are a few examples:
   a. You are an elite athlete who wants to go into coaching. Talk to your coach about what you need to begin learning and what he or she can allow you do to begin building skills.

b. You are a business executive who would like to do some consulting. Ask a former colleague who has already made that transition if you can join him or her on a consulting trip.

c. You are an athlete who believes you can leverage your name recognition to successfully sell insurance or real estate. Contact local agents to get recommendations for training classes or conferences you can attend and ask if you can tag along in the field.

d. You are a small business founder and owner who cares about education, and you are interested in volunteering for the school district you grew up in to help today's youngsters the same way you were helped. Create one evening each month to attend a local school board meeting to better understand the issues and how the district works to get things done.

There's another way to think about how practicing prepares you for retirement. Recall our discussion about the losses you will experience when you retire and the subsequent discussion about the phases of retirement. Managing through the transition phase is about taking steps to minimize the scope of the loss that you feel. If you plan and practice, you begin the process of coping earlier, reducing the gap between what was and what will be. Said another way, planning and practicing can shorten the time it takes you to get to the engagement phase, which is where you want to be.

2. <u>Revision (Game Plan Adjustment)</u>—Recall my former colleague's statement, "A plan is only something from which to deviate." It might sound as if he were dissing the value of planning, but he was simply emphasizing the reality that life circumstances are never constant, and it is better to have a plan when conditions do change rather than living with the chaos of having no prior direction.

Your life circumstances will change both before and after retirement. One of those changes might be that you thought there was something you would love to be doing in retirement, but it turns out not to be the case. Wouldn't you want to know that as early as possible, so you could change your retirement game plan to make the transition smoother? Practicing retirement will help you either confirm that your activity choices are right for you or that your game plan warrants change.

Recognize that each of the following examples are illustrations of success, not failure. Each one demonstrates that practice is valuable, and each of the retirees in the examples enters retirement much more confident in his or her plan for having practiced.

a. My friend, Keith, initially planned to do some teaching in retirement. While still working, he made arrangements to teach an evening class and found he hated it. The students were not paying attention, not doing the classwork, and still expecting A's. This was not consistent with Keith's values, nor was it a good use of his time. He changed his game plan prior to retirement.

b. You are a defensive lineman. Although long-distance running has never been part of your training regimen, you envision a retirement in which you lose weight and train for a marathon. During the off-season, you begin a running program, but you quickly learn that even at relatively short distances, your knees can't take the pounding. Change the game plan.

c. You are a physician in a one-person office. For decades, you've found it difficult to take more than a little time off. You and your spouse have talked about retirement plans and agree that you both want to see the world. You start practicing travel with some day trips and long weekends. You love it. Then you find someone to cover the office and free up ten days to practice retirement by taking a trip to London. And you hate it—the discomforts of travel make the trip difficult for you to enjoy, you don't like being so far from home and the grandchildren, and you are uncomfortable being away from aging parents. You have learned that shorter trips work best for you. Change the game plan.

d. You are a major leaguer who has always dreamed of becoming an author, and you even have ideas for several books. Writing is part of your retirement game plan. Although you may not begin working on your book while still playing, you practice by starting a blog. Despite fan interest, you find that sitting at the computer and writing is not for you. Taking on a book project with extended writing time would not likely be satisfying. Change the game plan.

125

3. <u>Financial Planning</u>—Financial advisors will tell you that they can do a much better job helping you with your retirement financial plan if you come to them with a well-thought-out retirement life game plan. If you have some reasonable certainty about what you are going to be doing and what your budget will likely be, you and your advisor can structure a financial plan that meets your needs. Practicing retirement, as described in points 1 and 2 above, will help you build confidence in your life game plan and by extension, enable you to build more confidence in your financial plan.

4. <u>Enjoyment</u>—The first three reasons should be compelling enough to have you want to practice retirement. To me, however, the most persuasive argument for practicing is that you will enhance the enjoyment of your life now. Why wait?

    Go back to the examples in point number 2 above. Each of these could have very well been examples accelerating living the dreams of retirement.

    a. If Keith had found he loved teaching, he would have had several years of additional enjoyment prior to retirement.

    b. Had the defensive lineman's knees tolerated long-distance running, he would have enjoyed training, increased distances, and entered retirement closer to his marathon dream.

    c. Had the physician and her spouse relished the trip to London, she would likely have found a way to take a few more international trips before retirement and entered retirement with a globetrotting plan.

    d. Had the major leaguer loved blogging, he would have likely begun to outline one of his book ideas while still playing, attended some writer's conferences in the off season, and spent some time reading about the writing craft.

    Part of the joy of practicing is the more-than-likely possibility that you'll love what you're doing. Don't wait—bring your exciting retirement dreams into your life—NOW!

Many retirees fall into the trap of believing that the best way to approach retirement is to take some significant time off to just chill and "figure it out later." Retirees of both generations report that this tactic is risky. The risk is that you will find yourself in a rut or very small comfort zone and have difficulty getting out of the transition stage and into full engagement. The benefits for a full and fulfilling retirement are too great to take the risk.

Regardless of where you are in your retirement journey, the best time to "figure it out" is now, and the best way to get started is to develop your game plan, then take steps to practice it.

a. If you want to do more volunteering (Giving Back), identify and talk to the right person at your place of worship, to a volunteer coordinator at your local United Way, or to friends who are giving of their time and talent— find something that fits your schedule.

b. If you want to build a broader network of friends outside your current circle of teammates or work colleagues (Healthy Relationships), find an evening a month to go out with that person who you enjoy being with but may not know as well as you'd like.

c. Similar to the physician and her husband in the example above, my wife and I knew we wanted to travel extensively in retirement (Fun, Passions, Growth). Five years before retiring, we started the "vacation-of-the-month" club. No, we didn't fly off to Hawaii every month. We took day trips, long weekends, and the occasional and affordable longer trip.

d. If you want to take up gardening, become a bridge master, develop a nonprofit that tutors reading for children, start that new business, or anything else that is on your retirement game plan activities list—bring a part or all of it into your life now.

When you are still playing or working in your career, sometimes finding time to fit something else in may seem difficult. Certainly you'll need to assess your schedule to make the time necessary to begin practicing.

As an elite athlete, you are busy, but are also likely to have some down time. How about in airports, on planes, in and around hotel rooms on road trips? You have your practice, travel, and game schedule for the season—do some scheduling well in advance to build in this important aspect of your life.

And how are you planning to spend the off season? Sure, you want to both give your body time to recover and to follow your off-season fitness regimen. But can't you also build in some retirement game plan practice time?

Let's summarize how this all fits together so far. You know that retirement is inevitable, and you can't be certain about when it will come. You want the next stage of your life to be meaningful. You have begun to think about how you are going to spend those coming years. You've completed an assessment of where you stand in your life today, and you've developed your retirement game plan.

Sure, you could wait until you actually retire, but there are so many compelling reasons to get ahead of that. You don't wait for game time in your sport to figure out what you're going to do. No, you anticipate and work to do what it takes in preparation to increase the odds of winning, including practice.

The same is true of retirement. Get ahead of it—start practicing now.

There's one final point to be made for practicing retirement in the inevitability phase. If your mindset is to find reasons not to plan and practice, I would argue that you haven't developed the attitude that will help make you successful in retirement.

People who are clicking on all cylinders in retirement are those who look for opportunities, recognize those opportunities, and are predisposed to say, "Yes." So, another thing to practice is just that; finding opportunities and saying "Yes" to them. Practicing retirement is an opportunity.

Is it different for the non-athlete professional who is approaching retirement? No. All of this applies to you as well. Go for it!

Practicing during the Transition and Engagement Phases

While the inevitability phase can be considered the practicing sweet spot, there is also a compelling way to think about also practicing retirement in the transition and engagement phases.

I've often wondered what it means to those who refer to themselves as having a medical, legal, architectural, accounting, dental, or other practice. I have a number of physicians and attorneys among my family members and friends, so to get some help thinking about this, I asked them why what they do is called "practicing."

The collective response was instructive. Not one of them had any idea. Here is some of what I got back from them.

"The origin of the term and exact meaning were certainly nothing I learned in medical school."

"It is just a term that is always used."

"Never thought about it."

"Just a guess."

"I have always thought the term was strange."

As it turns out, it's not strange at all, and its meaning has application in the context of retirement as well. To their credit, each one of them sought to help find an explanation, and we came across one that seemed to make sense.

An early definition in the Oxford English Dictionary for "practise" (British English spelling) included, "to pursue or be engaged in a particular occupation, profession, skill, or art."

While this is the definition that applies to practicing medicine or law, we could also argue that it applies to practicing retirement. I contend that retirement is not something we should simply live through until it's over. Rather it is a process we have control over, one with concepts to follow and with tools to use, one that we can constantly get better at, and one we can excel at.

Retirees can choose "to pursue" and "be engaged in a particular...skill." Isn't that what we're doing together as we go through the book? We're finding ways to pursue and be engaged in the skill of retirement—and maybe a bit of the "art" of retirement also.

When we practice retirement in the transition and engagement stages, we get better at it.

➤ We get better at developing our game plan and making game plan adjustments.

➤ We get better at living to our purpose and identifying our passions.

➤ We get better at holding ourselves accountable to make positive changes in our lives.

➤ We get better at developing healthy relationships, tending to our well-being, giving back to our communities, building our positive attitudes, keeping intellectually stimulated, and just plain having fun.

Retirement can be, should be, and is a wonderful time of reinvention, achievement, and winning. But it is a myth that retirement is easy. It takes mindfulness and persistent effort to continually improve who we are and the lives we are living.

Just as we respect those who practice medicine, law, architecture, and other professions, so should we respect those who practice retirement.

Pete Woods
NFL Quarterback
Practicing Law/Practicing Life

Balancing our careers with other aspects of life is both important and difficult. For elite athletes, this balancing act frequently begins at a very young age. Pete Woods' parents made sure that balance was a cornerstone at their home. Although they were supportive of his athletic pursuits, the former NFL quarterback was also expected to achieve academically. And his parents made sure that the value of giving back to his community was imbedded in the mix of his childhood expectations.

Pete admits that despite his parents' expectations and support, maintaining life balance was not easy. He excelled in both baseball and football at an early age, and much of his personal identity was built around athletic success. In high school, Pete was an All-State baseball pitcher and football quarterback. He was recognized as the most outstanding scholar-athlete in his area, and a local newspaper named him "High School Athlete of the Year."

Pete went on to quarterback the University of Missouri Tigers. He was second team All-Big 8 quarterback for two seasons and named to an All-America Team (top quarterback in the country among teams with losing records). Pete was being touted as a first-round NFL draft pick.

An elbow injury while pitching for Mizzou's baseball team and a football knee injury slowed him down, but not enough to prevent him from being drafted in the fourth round by the Kansas City Chiefs, beginning a four-year professional career as a backup quarterback for five teams. Pete's strength was his mobility, and an off-season knee injury in a pickup softball game heightened his awareness of the inevitability that he needed to be thinking about life-after-the-NFL.

Pete retired to begin law school and went on to become a well-recognized attorney. He is deeply involved in his church, is a community leader working for racial reconciliation, and is the vice-president of his local chapter of the NFL Retired Players Association.

Does he have regrets? Pete would love to have seen what might have happened had he been injury-free in college and during his pro career. But he is glad that he had heeded his parents' expectations. He feels fortunate to have been able to leverage his academics and commitment to giving back into a fulfilling post-sports career and life.

But he knows from his experience with the NFL Retired Players Association that his good fortune is not true for every former player. In fact, he observes, "not everyone prepared well for life-after-football." Many, if not most, players have neglected to focus on their future and have felt that somehow football would provide.

Chapter 8

When Should I Retire?

"The body says it's time, but within our hearts and minds we tell ourselves 'one more time.'
It's always one more time!"
Sugar Ray Leonard

"I knew it was time to retire when I was driving down the lane and got called for a three second violation."
Johnny "Red" Kerr

In his book, *The Way of Baseball: Finding Stillness at 95 MPH*, Shawn Green describes his retirement decision, which he made on a West Coast red-eye flight back to New York, where he lived with his wife and daughters and where he was playing for the Mets. At the time, Green was 34 years old and still productive, with the potential for more big-number years still in front of him, barring injury. These excerpts from the last chapter of his book help us see how Green was thinking through his decision:

- ➤ *"I'd made plenty of money, but retirement still meant passing on healthy paychecks."*
- ➤ *"I no longer had the intense drive to show everyone what I could do, to prove them all wrong. What did this mean? I wondered. Had I already let go, moved on?"*
- ➤ *"Surely, I loved baseball, but there were other things I loved, too. I missed my girls when I was away."*
- ➤ *"Whatever I decided about retirement, I knew I'd already fulfilled my baseball dream, and then some."*
- ➤ *"...more time with my family...what a fortunate man I was to have such options in the first place!"*

➤ *"I was excited to embrace the prospect of finding as heightened a state of awareness in my new life as I'd ever known when hitting a ninety-five mile per hour fastball with the sweet spot of my bat."*

Recall, retirement can result from injury, health issues, deselection, or personal choice. Green made the decision to retire on his own terms, just as did Bobby Jones, Rocky Marciano, Lorena Ochoa, and Jim Brown.

Four Questions

It is not my intent to suggest to anyone that retirement is right for them. But if you are trying to determine whether to retire on your own terms, there is an approach that can help. Simply, there are four questions to ask yourself, and when the answer to each question is "Yes," it is likely time for you to retire.

☐ **Do I have enough?**
☐ **Have I had enough?**
☐ **Will I have enough to do?**
☐ **Does my spouse/partner want me home 24/7?**

As you review the following details about each of the questions, come back and check the box if your answer is "Yes." Remember, these questions apply to the prospective retiree from any generation and occupation.

Do I have enough?
This is the question of whether you have a sufficient level of financial security. We reviewed earlier, "Financial security is not about how much money you have accumulated. Rather, it is about matching your lifestyle to your available resources. And for most, it is also about having a trusted, objective financial advisor on your team."

This checklist should get you well on your way to answering this question. Check the statement off if it is true for you.

☐ I understand my available resources.

☐ I have a good estimate about what I will be spending in retirement.

☐ I know what my short-term and long-term financial obligations are.

☐ I have gone through a thorough process of selecting my financial team, including a trusted advisor.

☐ I know whether I'll need to supplement my finances by working in retirement, and if so, I have a plan in place.

☐ I have a written financial plan that I understand and am comfortable with.

☐ If I have a spouse/partner, he or she also understands my written financial plan and is comfortable with it.

☐ Those closest to me understand and are aligned to how they fit into my retirement financial plan.

Let's spend a little more time on that last item. You'll note from these examples that it may be perfectly fine for you to be providing financial support for those closest to you, but that support needs to be built into your plan. The risks and benefits must be fully understood, and your choices and expectations shared with those affected.

➤ Have you been supporting family and friends throughout your athletic career? Will that continue?

➤ As an older non-athlete, are you financially supporting aging parents and/or adult children? If not, do you anticipate the need to do so in the future?

➤ The media is rife with stories of "friends" of athletes pitching get-rich-quick schemes and asking the athlete to invest. Has a friend come to you with a proposal for you to buy into a can't-miss investment? Do you have a way to consider the proposal holistically, if this happens to you? You may want to revisit the "Critical Decision Making" planning tool in Chapter 5.

Before we move on, we have an opportunity to connect two concepts to further help you answer the question, "Do I have enough?" Large signing bonuses and salaries may have you, as an elite athlete, steeped in the habit of large spending. If that spending continues in retirement, it may not bode well. This is an area ripe for "practicing retirement." As you consider deciding whether you will "have enough," begin downsizing your spending during your career.

Connecting financial planning and practicing is appropriate for non-athlete professionals as well. Have you aligned your spending habits while still working with what you will need your retirement habits to be?

Do I have enough? Yes? No?

Have I had enough?

There is absolutely nothing wrong with continuing to play/work, if you are still energized and fulfilled. When Jason Giambi was 43 and the oldest player in major league baseball at the time, he had not had enough and was doing acupuncture to stay in the game. "I'm older and traveling a lot and not sleeping so much," Giambi said. "We got on this routine of doing acupuncture...and it's made a huge difference for me."

There may be a time, however, when despite having had a successful and passionate career, it no longer lights your fire. If that is the case for you, then the answer to this question might be "Yes."

You're a 58-year old teacher who has had a wonderful career, but you realize you're just not energized as you once were to get up in the morning, get to school, and face the classroom.

You're Sandy Koufax, "I've got a lot of years to live after baseball; I would like to live them with complete use of my body. I don't regret a minute of the last 12 years, but I think I would regret a one year that was too many."

You're a 62-year old executive, and every business problem feels like you've-been-there-done-that; the passion is gone.

You're Shawn Green, "I no longer had the intense drive to show everyone what I could do, to prove them all wrong. What did this mean? I wondered. Had I already let go, moved on?"

This second retirement decision-making question is typically easy to answer. You'll know it when you feel it. Have I had enough? Yes? No?

Will I have enough to do?

This question tends to be harder to answer than the last one. Perhaps another way to ask it is, "Do I have a retirement game plan that excites me?" The key here is to recognize that although you may have answered question 2 with "Yes," the magic is if you are not just retiring *from* something, but *to* something.

If you haven't even gotten a substantial start on your retirement game plan, it will likely be difficult for you to answer, "Will I have enough to do?" Here are some questions, derived from the planning tools we reviewed earlier, to help you decide if this is a "Yes" or "No."

➢ Do I have a compelling bucket list? Is it written? Am I thinking about what to add to it? Am I completing items?

➢ Do I have a written retirement game plan? Does it include things I want to start, stop, and continue in my life? Is it holistic in that it brings all of the ten key elements of a fulfilling retirement into my life?

➢ Have I identified my passions, what I love to do? Have I identified my strengths, what I am great at? Have I identified what the world needs, especially as it relates to my community, that I can help with? Have I brought all of those together to find the magic and add to the meaningful things I'll be doing?

➢ Have I identified my ideal day, week, and year to give me yet another retirement game planning target to strive for?

Will I have enough to do? Yes? No?

Does my spouse/partner want me home 24/7?

Having read the book to this point, you should be well-convinced that it is important to have discussed your retirement plan with those closest to you, especially your spouse or partner. Have you had the "crucial conversations" with them?

Part of your assessment of this question is based on your sensitivity to their plan as well. Have you asked them about, discussed, and aligned to their plan? Recall, the best scenario is when:

> ➤ You have a retirement game plan and those closest to you are aligned.
> ➤ Your spouse or partner has a retirement game plan to which you are aligned.
> ➤ Your spouse or partner and you have a joint plan that you both agree to.

Does my spouse/partner want me home 24/7? Yes? No?

In 2014, at the age of 34, following a successful and healthy season at offensive tackle with the Carolina Panthers, the only professional team he played for in 11-year NFL career, Jordan Gross retired by personal choice.

Do I have enough? "Oh, I thought about that. Who wouldn't? It's really great, to have all that money. But how good would it be to play a year or two more and have that extra money, and you have a shot joint or a knee that doesn't work anymore? I made a lot of money playing football already." Yes. Check.

Have I had enough? "I never wanted to play longer than I should. I never wanted anyone to be able to say, 'He stayed too long.' Instead of just hanging on and playing at a lower level, I always thought it would be better for people to say to me, 'Why'd you retire? You were great last year.'" Yes. Check.

Will I have enough to do? He spent two years as the sideline reporter for the Panthers game broadcasts. He has left that work, "I just want to spend time with my family. I loved the opportunity. I love the Panthers. I just want to have more availability, try some new stuff in life." Yes. Check.

Does my spouse want me home 24/7? He turned down opportunities to join Fortune 500 companies to be sure he was home with family more, and they're happy with that. As soon as the school year was over for the kids, the family took a long trip together to the Oregon coast. Yes. Check.

✓ **Do I have enough?**
✓ **Have I had enough?**
✓ **Will I have enough to do?**
✓ **Does my spouse/partner want me home 24/7?**

Gross retired on his own terms and is happy with his decision, "You know how I know I made the right decision? I haven't thought once that I did the wrong thing. Not once."

Cindy Rarick
Professional Golfer
"I began to see the writing on the wall."

Professional golf may be the sport for which the average retirement age is the oldest. And it is a sport for which there can be and is a tour for "seniors." In the case of the LPGA, there is a Legends Tour that conducts an abbreviated number of events for which players over the age of 45 are eligible. That being said, studies have shown that the peak years for golfers are generally between 30 and 35, after which tournament results decline rapidly.

An example of golf career longevity is Cindy Rarick, who played on the LPGA tour from 1985 until 2008, when she was 48. Cindy began playing and winning early, being a Junior and Women's champion in Arizona and Hawaii, respectively, before the age of 20. The winning continued through her professional career; five US tournament wins and one international championship. She surpassed $2,000,000 in prize money at the age of 43.

Cindy ascribes her success and longevity to discipline and believes that trait is necessary for every elite athlete. It takes discipline to consistently practice, to stay in physical shape, and to eat nutritiously in the face of potential distractions. Cindy traveled extensively during her career, having flown more than 3,000,000 miles on one airline alone. She's been to Japan over 50 times, to Australia more than ten, and to Europe more than that. The rigors of travel, the difficulty of getting enough sleep, the challenge to eat the right foods and not too much of them are but some of the issues that make discipline important.

All of this became more difficult as Cindy aged through her career. Eventually, she encountered a mechanical problem with her swing that no amount of coaching and practice could fix. As her scores suffered and she was no longer in the competitive groupings, Cindy became frustrated. She had been so excited about playing her entire career that she invariably jumped out of bed in the morning and could not wait to get to the driving range and course. With her swing in disarray and her scores soaring, the fun had disappeared. She says, "I began to see the writing on the wall."

How did Cindy answer the four questions and why?

1. **Do I have enough?** Yes. Cindy had realized early in her career that being smart with her money would be important. She had applied her tour winnings to real estate, equities, and other sound investments that put her in good stead. She also received a $170,000 lifetime pension from the LPGA. Although this amount is orders of magnitude less than the male PGA players get and less than that of other sports, it added to her retirement fund.

2. **Have I had enough?** Yes. Swing problems. High scores. Being noncompetitive. Having little fun. It just was not the experience that she was used to having on the golf course. Time to move on.

3. **Will I have enough to do?** Yes. Cindy knew she had a number of things other than golf that she was interested in, but she also knew that she would want to stay connected to her game. Some of her fellow retired competitors were teaching golf or had opened academies when they retired. Cindy chose not to take that route but decided to play recreationally and in some of the Legends Tour events. She finds the events fun, an opportunity to make a little extra income, and a chance to participate in clinics to help youngsters enjoy the game. But her new passion is the winery she began with her partner, Gary Seidler. Silvara Vineyards is in the state of Washington, where Cindy spends her summers while spending her winters in Arizona.

4. **Does my partner want me around 24/7?** Yes. Cindy and Gary had talked about their winery venture. They were looking forward to doing it together and leaving the tour enabled Cindy to join Gary, something they both looked forward to—together.

Playing the Game

You have likely learned that regardless of how well you prepare for a game or meet or tournament or class or client or patient, your ability to adjust to unpredictably changing circumstances is one key to being successful at whatever your profession.

Similarly, one of the certainties of retirement is that life circumstances will change. In large regard, the quality of our lives is contingent on how well we recognize and adjust to those changing circumstances. Are we resilient? Are we willing to acknowledge the reality that things have changed? Are we able to deviate from our game plan, establish our new plan, and move on?

I'll refer us to my former colleague's profound statement one final time, "A plan is only something from which to deviate."

His teaching has four components: 1) have a plan, 2) anticipate there will be changing circumstances, 3) make the necessary adjustments to your plan, and 4) proceed with confidence.

In these final chapters, we're going to do two things. First, we'll discuss the value of making adjustments when they're needed. Second, we'll summarize the key points and overall approach to make sure that when we put it all together, we win.

Chapter 9

Making Adjustments

*"I have a plan of action,
but the game is a game of adjustments."*
Mike Krzyzewski

"Life is what happens while you're busy making other plans."
John Lennon

One of the tools we reviewed for developing your plan was "Game Plan Adjustments." It complements the other five tools, because there is no doubt that you will need to make adjustments to account for changing life circumstances, whether they be positive or negative. Here are a few examples:

> ➤ You plan to retire in several years but an injury accelerates the schedule.
> ➤ You have completed bucket list items and added exciting new ones.
> ➤ You confront illness, either yours or someone close to you.
> ➤ You have changes in your family dynamics—children or grandchildren are born, you get married, or you experience a divorce.
> ➤ As an older non-athlete, you have adult children move back home. If you are a retiring athlete, you may be that adult child.
> ➤ The stock market takes a significant turn for the better or the worse.
> ➤ You get a call from a friend that starts out something like, "Wow, do I ever have a deal for you."
> ➤ You discover a new passion in your life, or you lose interest in something you thought you were passionate about.

"The best laid plans…"

October 15, 2015—Jets at the Patriots. Early in the game, the Jets show a pressure formation with seven men on the defensive line of scrimmage, and they bring them all, adding the safety on a late blitz. Bill Belichick and Tom Brady learn from that and make a game plan adjustment.

Fourth quarter—Jets show the same defensive formation. The original plan was to hold tight end Rob Gronkowski in to block when the Jets showed pressure. Adjustment—the Patriots release Gronk instead of holding him in to block—quick pass, 15-yard catch and run—touchdown. Patriots 30; Jets 23.

"The best laid plans of mice and men often go astray." The statement changed a bit since it was first written in 1785 by Scotsman Robert Burns in his poem, "To a Mouse," (original: "The best laid schemes o' mice an' men; Gang aft a-gley.") yet it has application today in our retirement context.

➤ About the same time we retired, my wife and I had our first grandchild, a very positive development in our lives (thank you Dana and Vince). Jordan was in St. Louis, where we had grown up, but we then lived in Cincinnati. When he was born, we began traveling to St. Louis one week each month, and we eventually realized it was time to move to St. Louis, which we did. We adjusted our plan.

➤ Kareem Abdul-Jabbar, the all-time career NBA scoring leader, was active in retirement, including writing a number of books, when he was diagnosed with chronic myeloid leukemia, a blood cancer that he manages with drug therapy. Not only did he need to build therapy into his plan, but he also became a spokesperson for Novartis Pharmaceuticals and began giving back by becoming a patient listener to those who wanted to share their stories. And, by the way, Abdul-Jabbar frequently writes about retirement life planning. He adjusted his plan.

➤ Darryl Strawberry fought a wide range of demons, both during his 17-year major league baseball career and in retirement. During a recovery convention organized by Narcotics Anonymous, Strawberry was introduced to Tracy Boulware. They fell in love, married, and founded Strawberry Ministries. He/they adjusted the plan.

➤ In 1999, three years before I retired, I realized that arthritis had begun to settle into my hips. Over the years, I played baseball in my senior leagues and tournaments in more and more pain, and the issue eventually had a significant effect on the quality of my daily life. In 2013, I had both of my hips replaced. Because I had a diverse portfolio of retirement activities in my plan, I was able to give up playing baseball and focus on other things. That being said, after sitting out of baseball that year, I was glad when the doctor said that I was able to return to playing the game, and I did so, with no pain and with full range of motion. I adjusted my plan—several times.

➤ Dorothy Hamill, Olympic gold-medal figure skater, has had a full and fulfilling retirement since she left her sport in 1976. Yet during that timeframe, she has had to deal with osteoarthritis, and she was diagnosed and treated for breast cancer. She continues to remain active and for both diseases, Hamill stepped up to become a visible spokesperson to help others cope with their diagnoses. She adjusted her plan.

➤ George Foreman retired at age 28 from a heavyweight boxing career during which he was both an Olympic gold medalist and professional World Champion. Ten years later, he found himself unable to afford supporting his family or keeping his Houston youth center open. Foreman returned to the ring at age 38 and 50 pounds heavier. During this improbable comeback, he regained his title at age 45 and became the oldest heavyweight champ in history. Foreman retired for the second time at age 48. He had adjusted his plan.

Should we have a retirement game plan? Yes.

Will our best-laid plans go astray? Yes

Will things change in our lives in the same way they change during an athletic contest or business situation? Yes.

Will those changes sometimes be negative and sometimes positive? Yes.

Should we acknowledge those changes and adjust our game plan? Yes.

Dan Cross
Professional Basketball Player
"Turn the lights back on"

Dan Cross has made adjustments both during and after his professional basketball career.

Through youth basketball, Carbondale Community High School, the University of Florida, and professional teams in ten countries, Dan Cross pursued his life-long dream of playing in the NBA. Although he never made it to that top level of his profession, to this day, he feels fortunate to have had the playing career he did.

Dan was a two-time honorable mention All-American point guard at Florida, where in the 1993-94 season, he averaged a team-high 15.7 points per game and led the Gators to their first-ever Final Four appearance. After being surprised and disappointed not to have been picked in the 1995 draft, he paused and thought about hanging up his sneakers, but Dan did a "gut check" and opted to stay the course with a full focus on pursuing a pro basketball career.

After trying to make several NBA teams but being cut late in the process, he elected to move on to play internationally. Dan was driven to create a solid financial and lifestyle foundation for his future, both for himself and for an eventual family. And he wanted to take full advantage of the opportunity and of his basketball skills to "dictate to life before it dictated to him." Although initially feeling well out of his comfort zone by living abroad, he eventually enjoyed playing for teams in Greece, Italy, Turkey, Finland, Venezuela, and other countries.

Then, playing for an Israeli team at age 33, Dan tore an Achilles tendon. While recovering from the injury in Israel, he was inspired by the country and its biblical history to move on with his life versus trying to resurrect his career. It was time to quit missing Christmases, Thanksgivings, birthdays, and other important times in his life and the lives of loved ones—something he had been doing because of tournaments and league schedules since he was 13 years old. Dan decided that his new path in life needed to be one of gratitude for the years of basketball he had and for the opportunity to give back to others.

Fortunately, Dan had begun to think about what he wanted to do post-career while he was still playing. He had begun to run basketball camps during the summers, and he recognized the need for student-athletes to acquire life skills many of them did not have. He began a foundation to work with these student-athletes.

But he knew nothing of running an organization and viewed it as needing to "learn how to dribble all over again." He had started his non-athletic career later in life than his age-group peers without the skills and background to be successful. When he tried to find a job, his resume was filled with basketball teams for which he had played but not with skills and experiences he could offer employers.

Despite knowing what he wanted to do with his life, transition from his athletic career proved difficult, and as Dan says, "It came at a great cost." The people around him did not understand why he could not adjust to the transition. He was confronting the need to make financial and lifestyle changes; he was fighting not to succumb to emotional swings; and he was trying to answer the questions, "Now that basketball is over, what am I passionate about and what am I good at?"

The stress of the transition cost him his marriage of ten years and led to bouts of depression. He was sometimes finding it difficult to get out of bed in the morning and constantly thinking, "I no longer have basketball—I'm not going to be successful anymore." He knew that he needed to find a new passion if he were to "turn the lights back on."

That new passion is Athletes Connection, which he founded and leads—it is "dedicated to assisting current and former student-athletes in finding careers and making the transition from athletics to the workforce." Dan finds meaning in his work and is energized by being able to use his experience to give back to others and by seeing the results of making a difference in the lives of the young people with whom he works. Dan's lights are back on.

When to Make Adjustments

Responding to changing life circumstances is one time to make retirement game plan adjustments, but there are other indicators as well.

One of these indicators is if you find that things that used to excite you no longer do; a phenomenon that is not uncommon.

A classic goes something like this. You run into an acquaintance who is approaching retirement and ask him what he plans to do after the big day comes. He sports a big smile and says, "I'm really looking forward to it. I'm going to play golf every day!" Big emphasis on "every."

Then you run into him about six months later. "So, how is retirement going?"

"Oh, it's OK."

"How are you spending your time?"

Shoulder shrug, "I'm playing some golf." Emphasis on "some."

Recall the "Find the Magic" game planning tool. It is the tool designed to help you identify what you are good at, what the world needs that you can help with, and what you love to do. If what you love to do has become less exciting, then the magic can wear off. When that happens, it is likely time, perhaps well past time, to adjust your plan.

By the way, one way to prevent you from losing interest in something you are passionate about is to have a diverse portfolio of meaningful activities in your game plan. You'll still be able to enjoy your passion, but you will have ensured that you are not single-mindedly focused on just that one thing.

Another indicator that your plan may need an adjustment is the size of your bucket list. When most people put their written bucket lists together for the first time, their list of items is fairly extensive. That's great. You begin checking items off your list. And you occasionally add other items, but the risk is that you check off faster than you replace.

It might be time, again perhaps past time, to adjust your plan by working on replenishing your bucket list. Ask friends and acquaintances what's on their lists. Check social media to see what people are doing that excites them. Add items that excite you to your list. Remember, the items don't have to be big undertakings; smaller items can be as energizing and perhaps easier to plan and do.

Remember the "transition phase" of retirement, that time when you experience a wide range of emotions as you deal with what you lost when you retired? We also said that it would not be uncommon for those mixed emotions to come back periodically. When they do, it's possible that you'll feel some level of disenchantment. You might find yourself spending more and more time in front of the TV. Perhaps you find yourself becoming more and more isolated—spending more days at home than out and about.

If you find yourself in this situation, do all you can to reengage with life, and a good way to do this is to take out your written game plan and make sure it's serving you well. Are you still doing those things that you identified you wanted to "continue" to do? Are there different things that should be on your "start" list? Do you need to adjust your plan?

Let's summarize the indicators of when it's time to adjust your game plan:

1. Life circumstances have changed significantly, either positively or negatively
2. Some of the things that used to excite you have lost their edge; the "magic" is fading
3. Your written bucket list is low on items
4. You are feeling disenchanted with life and symptoms of isolation and ennui are settling in

And the final suggestion on when it's time to review and perhaps adjust your plan is when you haven't changed it for a while, like maybe in the past three months. You may not find it necessary to make a change, but it can't hurt to check. Take it out and do a quick review to make sure you're on track toward living the retirement you deserve.

Chapter 10

Winning

"I love the winning, I can take the losing,
But most of all I love to play."
Boris Becker

"Winning is only half of it.
Having fun is the other half."
Bum Phillips

Did you know the vast majority of the books on people's bookshelves go unopened or unfinished? So, congratulations to us both—you've made it this far, and I've helped keep you interested enough to do so.

Putting It All Together

Let's take all of the concepts and tools we've covered and put them all together using the "5-P's," Preparing, Planning, Practicing, Partnering, and Playing.

You've worked your way through the book and are much better positioned to develop and live the retirement you dream of. You've worked hard to get to this point in your life, and you deserve to reap the benefits. Will it always be easy? No. But if you invest your time and energy to follow this process, you will increase the odds of winning in retirement.

This 5-P structure introduces no new concepts or tools. Rather it provides you with just one more way to think about what is in front of you and how to approach it, using the concepts and tools you've already learned about earlier in the book.

Preparing for Retirement:

➤ Become aware of what retirement is and is not (Chapter 1)

➤ Understand what you will lose when you leave your career and how those losses might affect you (Chapter 2)

➤ Recognize that retirement is inevitable and that preparing for that eventuality will put you in good stead for working your way through the phases of retirement (Chapter 3)

Planning for Retirement:

➤ Assess your strengths and weaknesses relative to the ten key elements of a fulfilling retirement; then use that assessment as a foundation for your retirement plan (Chapter 4)

➤ Use the practical, simple, and proven tools to develop your retirement game plan (Chapter 5)

➤ If you have the capability to retire on your own terms, determine when you should take that step (Chapter 8)

Practicing Retirement:

➤ Bring your retirement dreams and plans into your life today, even while you are still playing/working—this will help you confirm your game plan, establish a more robust financial plan, make your transition into retirement much smoother, and, importantly, enhance your life today (Chapter 7)

Partnering in Retirement:

➤ Identify and recruit your retirement support team to make sure you have the resources and personal relationships you'll need to be successful (Chapter 6)

➤ Have the crucial conversations with those close to you to ensure they are aware of and aligned with your retirement plans (Chapter 6)

Playing the Retirement Game:

➤ Use your game plan to do the things you have chosen to do in retirement; then acknowledge that life circumstances will change and you will need to make game plan adjustments (Chapter 9)

➤ Whether you are an elite athlete or anyone who has dedicated yourself to building a winning career, you have earned the right to also be a winner in retirement, *After the Cheering Stops*.

Made in the USA
San Bernardino, CA
07 February 2018